Birthday Secrets

What the Date of Your Birth Reveals About You

Jill M. Phillips is the author of dozens of books and hundreds of articles on astrology. She has regularly written forecast columns for *Astrology: Your Daily Horoscope* and has contributed to *Globe*'s mini-magazine astrology series. Ms. Phillips works with clients through Moon Dancer AstroGraphics, her astrological counseling service.

Cover Illustration: Shutterstock

Interior Illustrations: PIL Collection, Shutterstock

Copyright © 2013 Publications International, Ltd. All rights reserved. This book may not be reproduced or quoted in whole or in part by any means whatsoever without written permission from:

Louis Weber, CEO
Publications International, Ltd.
7373 North Cicero Avenue
Lincolnwood, Illinois 60712

Permission is never granted for commercial purposes.

ISBN-13: 978-1-4508-6324-7
ISBN-10: 1-4508-6324-8

Manufactured in USA.

8 7 6 5 4 3 2 1

The Goat

January 1 · Capricorn · You have an aristocratic nature.
You demonstrate good taste in all aspects of life and know how to live well, even on limited resources. You expect a great deal of yourself and always strive to live up to your full potential. This attitude translates to a search for personal excellence, which can be rewarding but also exhausting, since you tend to be a perfectionist. You have regal appeal and attract special attention in love and romance. You possess strong powers of patience and endurance and understand that some goals take a long time to achieve.

AVOID: Being overly sensitive; emotional isolation; anxiety

ALSO BORN ON THIS DAY: Baseball star Hank Greenberg; actor Frank Langella; novelist J. D. Salinger

ↄ

January 2 · Capricorn · Secretive and quiet, you present a
stern face to the world. This persona belies your actual nature, which is considerably more animated and joyous. A sense of being judged by others keeps you from revealing your sensitivity to all but your closest friends. You seek quality, not quantity, in friendship and tend to cultivate a small circle of close friends. A certain level of personal detachment allows you to behave as a spectator to your own actions, learning from each experience. You don't credit others for your success, but neither do you blame anyone for your failures. Don't let the possibility of failure keep you from pursuing your dreams.

AVOID: Melancholy; self-pity; being contemptuous of others

ALSO BORN ON THIS DAY: Writer Isaac Asimov; actor Cuba Gooding Jr.; supermodel Christy Turlington

ↄ

The Goat

January 3 · Capricorn · You are resourceful and able
to draw good things into your life without exerting much effort.
You have a streak of originality, which is always evident in your
personality and your work. You are naturally acquisitive: Material
objects are important to you, but only as an outward expression of
how you feel about your circumstances and the world around you.
You often have difficulty expressing your true feelings, even to those
closest to you. Your aspirations are endless. After you achieve one
goal, you turn your attention to the next one. You never set any
limits on what you can do, and because of this you usually succeed!

AVOID: Being secretive; self-indulgence; distractions

ALSO BORN ON THIS DAY: Hockey star Bobby Hull; activist
Lucretia Mott; writer J.R.R. Tolkien

January 4 · Capricorn · You possess a quirky, mercurial
personality. You are dedicated to acts of kindness on a personal
level, acts of humanity on a public level. You are extremely issue-
oriented and are not shy about expressing your opinions. You have
a heartfelt sympathy for the unfortunate, and you feel it is your duty
to draw attention to the plight of such people. You are not merely
opinionated—you are extremely vocal about your opinions and try
to speak the truth. Your primary desire is to experience life in all its
variety. You want to see and do things that most people miss.

AVOID: Transgressions; irreverence; pessimism

ALSO BORN ON THIS DAY: Inventor Louis Braille; writer Jacob
Grimm; football coach Don Shula

The Goat

January 5 · Capricorn · You have strong opinions but don't expect your friends to always agree with you—in fact, you appreciate a rowdy debate now and then. You are fascinated by small details and large events—the whole pattern of human existence.

AVOID: Boredom; pressure; complaints

ALSO BORN ON THIS DAY: Actor Robert Duvall; novelist Umberto Eco; actor Diane Keaton

January 6 · Capricorn · Contrary to most Capricorn natives, you are totally uninhibited. You refuse to be bound by the rules of convention, though you have an innate sense of decorum that allows you to be rebellious in the most courteous way possible. You make your own rules, and you are quite charming.

AVOID: Defenses; obsessions; intrigue

ALSO BORN ON THIS DAY: Heroine Joan of Arc; writer Carl Sandburg; filmmaker John Singleton

January 7 · Capricorn · You have a vulnerability that endears you to others. You have a strong spiritual nature as well as a social conscience, and you are often drawn into political activism or humanitarian concerns. You are likely to experience a conflict between your inner-life needs and your external responsibilities.

AVOID: Transient affections; impermanence; confusion

ALSO BORN ON THIS DAY: *The New Yorker* cartoonist Charles Addams; actor Nicolas Cage; writer Zora Neale Hurston

The Goat

January 8 · Capricorn ·
You seek to balance worldly concerns with an expression of your own needs. Although you strive for a pragmatic approach to life, you have an extremely superstitious nature. It's important to you that you are in control of your own destiny. Although you are very gifted, you may be riddled with self-doubts and profound questions about the nature of your place in the universe. These problems are exacerbated by the fact that you have difficulty expressing your feelings through words. You are noted for your loyalty and generosity. While you may dream big dreams, your true goal is to understand your own motivations.

AVOID: Overindulgence; greed; self-pity

ALSO BORN ON THIS DAY: Musician David Bowie; theoretical physicist Stephen Hawking; musician Elvis Presley

January 9 · Capricorn ·
You are a complicated person and may seem to be at war with yourself at times. Brilliant and philosophical, you often strain to maintain a facade to appeal to others. You reach for the stars, striving for perfection on every level. You are a tireless worker and are willing to sacrifice a great deal to prove your worth. You are ambitious and hardworking, and you often are content to sacrifice personal happiness in order to achieve career desires. Despite your very private nature, you have a great need to attract public notice. When you transcend your shyness, you may experience your most ambitious and satisfying successes.

AVOID: Hypocrisy; extravagance; dishonesty

ALSO BORN ON THIS DAY: Musician Joan Baez; writer Simone de Beauvoir; Kate Middleton, Duchess of Cambridge

The Goat

January 10 · Capricorn ·

People born on January 10 have heightened perception and fiercely held likes and dislikes. You are strong-minded and are not shy about dealing with others in a direct manner. You have no secret agenda: You are proud of your forthright approach to life and may even flaunt it at times. Your swaggering attitude attracts others to you—you have the ability to make others see things through your eyes, change opinions, and change lives. Although your approach to projects may be somewhat unorthodox, you can think and act on the fly. You always manage to get the job done and have a sense of urgency about everything you do.

Avoid: Antagonism; pretense; misdirection

Also born on this day: Musician Pat Benatar; sculptor Barbara Hepworth; actor Sal Mineo

♑

January 11 · Capricorn ·

You possess great personal dignity. You are a lovable person, yet you have a tendency to be inflexible where philosophy is concerned. Attractive and personable, you are also brilliant—a fact you may hide to gain leverage. You have the ability to rise from seeming obscurity to achieve everything you desire. Your intractable determination is by far your most remarkable characteristic. You're unlikely to be swept off your feet, since practicality dominates most of your decisions. You feel that struggle enhances accomplishment. You understand that some goals take a great deal of time to achieve, but you have a lot of patience.

Avoid: Patronizing attitude; coldness; aloofness

Also born on this day: Musician Clarence Clemons; American patriot Alexander Hamilton; philosopher William James

♑

The Goat

January 12 · Capricorn ·

You enjoy giving the impression that you are far more adventuresome than you are. You possess a good sense of humor. Bold and imaginative, you have an intellectual sophistication that few people can appreciate, and you go to great lengths to prove your abilities.

AVOID: Self-delusion; riding the moral high horse; incompetence

ALSO BORN ON THIS DAY: Actor Kirstie Alley; Amazon.com founder Jeff Bezos; writer Jack London

January 13 · Capricorn ·

Fearless, reckless, eager to meet all of life's challenges—you often lead a tumultuous existence. You can see the funny side of any situation. You have the power to learn from your mistakes, and if you are unable to envision failure, it's because you are stubborn as well as optimistic.

AVOID: Failure; tedium; short-sightedness

ALSO BORN ON THIS DAY: Writer Horatio Alger; actor Julia Louis-Dreyfus; dancer Gwen Verdon

January 14 · Capricorn ·

You are happiest juggling a variety of responsibilities. Scholarly and verbal, you recognize your own limitations. You set high standards for yourself, yet you take disappointment without losing your enthusiasm.

AVOID: Acrimony; an arrogant attitude; sanctimonious behavior

ALSO BORN ON THIS DAY: Novelist John Dos Passos; actor Faye Dunaway; humanitarian Albert Schweitzer

The Goat

January 15 · **Capricorn** · Although you wear the mask of practicality with conviction, you have a complicated nature. You want to create a legacy. You seek comfort at every level of existence and are equally concerned with maintaining the comfort of others. Physically, emotionally, and spiritually, you do what you can to make the world a better place. You gravitate toward good feelings, good works, and good intentions. While you enjoy living in the lap of luxury, you never lose sight of the intangible virtues that truly make life worth living. You tend to be a loner, but you possess a special magnetism that draws people to you effortlessly.

AVOID: Feeling blue; secret agendas; possessiveness

ALSO BORN ON THIS DAY: Actor Lloyd Bridges; civil rights leader Martin Luther King Jr.; actor/filmmaker Mario Van Peebles

January 16 · **Capricorn** · Although you have the temperament of a loner, you love people. You have the capacity to indulge your materialistic needs without losing sight of the importance of spirituality in your life. Something of an enigma to all who know you, you have an inner intensity that fuels all your actions. You connect with others on many levels, and you want to be challenged by your friends. When you use your considerable imaginative power and creativity and set your sights upon achievement, you have the heart to stick with it. You enjoy spending money on beautiful things, and you are very generous.

AVOID: Escapism; irrational behavior; detachment

ALSO BORN ON THIS DAY: Dancer/choreographer Debbie Allen; filmmaker John Carpenter; writer Susan Sontag

The Goat

January 17 · Capricorn · You grasp the correlation

between mental and physical energy. You're devoted to the notion of "peak experience." You operate on a level of almost primal instinct, trusting your intuition in almost every situation. You continually put yourself "out there" in order to prove yourself.

AVOID: Vanity; negativity; adulation

ALSO BORN ON THIS DAY: Comedian Jim Carrey; American patriot Benjamin Franklin; actor Betty White

January 18 · Capricorn · With you, the accent is always on

personal charisma. You can charm just about anyone, and you have the potential to be extremely manipulative. In most instances you are forthright. You crave excitement and variety.

AVOID: Limitations; loneliness; struggle

ALSO BORN ON THIS DAY: Actor Cary Grant; comedian Oliver Hardy; writer A. A. Milne

January 19 · Capricorn · You recognize the strong

connection between conscious and unconscious thought, which come together in dreams and creativity. You have an excellent grasp of worldly wisdom. You are eager for success and are wise enough to look to valued friends and associates for assistance.

AVOID: Superficiality; insecurity; holding grudges

ALSO BORN ON THIS DAY: Artist Paul Cézanne; musician Janis Joplin; author/poet Edgar Allan Poe

The Water Bearer

January 20 · **Aquarius** · You have a quiet determination
that gets you through difficult times, and you tend to be concerned
about the image you project. You are broad-minded about love and
sexuality but have a certain cynicism about romance. You have a
strong determination to succeed, and if you're able to follow your
intuition, you can be amazingly successful. You feel as if you were
chosen to do something special in the world. Few people learn more
from their mistakes than you do.

AVOID: Routine; defeatism; judgmental individuals

ALSO BORN ON THIS DAY: Astronaut Buzz Aldrin; comedian
George Burns; comedian Bill Maher

January 21 · **Aquarius** · Cool on the outside, you possess a
magnetism that puts you in the spotlight. Although you may appear
somewhat egotistical, you are a generous soul. Sexual, spiritual,
intelligent, and fun-loving, you can see the humor in things—even
yourself. You are more conventional in romantic matters than many
Aquarians. You are interested in marriage rather than the pursuit
of a series of relationships. You may have some difficulty working
for others—perfectionism is part of the problem. It's necessary
for you to have many goals in order to keep you from becoming
directionless. You need to understand that it is your own best
efforts—not success—that crown your achievement.

AVOID: Danger; unpreparedness; surprise

ALSO BORN ON THIS DAY: Fashion designer Christian Dior; Civil
War General Thomas "Stonewall" Jackson; golf star Jack Nicklaus

The Water Bearer

January 22 · Aquarius · You are talented and tend to call

attention to yourself, enjoying being the focus of any group. Able to
find the uniqueness in each experience, you enjoy the resonance of
negative as well as positive emotions. You are typically attracted to
glamorous types who mirror your own dark side. You may spend
years developing your talents, and you always believe in yourself,
even if few others do. When rewarded for hard work, you aren't
content to revel in your good fortune. You set new standards for
yourself, new heights to reach.

AVOID: Lies; denial; self-neglect

ALSO BORN ON THIS DAY: Musician Sam Cooke; poet George
Gordon, Lord Byron; celebrity chef Guy Fieri

January 23 · Aquarius · You're a hard-headed realist;

a strong, silent type. There's a toughness about you that's at once
laudable and useful: You seem able to handle anything. Inside,
you're a tender soul. You hesitate to complain, and you hide your
vulnerabilities for fear you'll be considered weak. Often put in the
position of role model, you do not generally regard your conduct as
anything special. You are motivated to achieve career success and
may not realize until late that you also want personal stability. You
want to be the best at what you do. You take criticism well and are
able to look at yourself objectively.

AVOID: Excessive solitude; being antisocial; grudges

ALSO BORN ON THIS DAY: Monaco's Princess Caroline; American
patriot John Hancock; actor Mariska Hargitay

January 24 · Aquarius · You feel a need to shock those closest to you. Beneath the surface, you are kind and have a genuine love for others. You have the potential to do amazing things but may require the validation of others to believe in yourself.

AVOID: Making demands; physical excesses; risks

ALSO BORN ON THIS DAY: Comedian John Belushi; musician Neil Diamond; Olympian Mary Lou Retton

January 25 · Aquarius · Dreamy and introspective, you have intelligence and charm, as well as a profound sense of your own destiny. Commitment is not easy for you; you tend to idealize love. To make romance work, you need to come down to earth.

AVOID: Fair-weather friends; petty dislikes; crankiness

ALSO BORN ON THIS DAY: Poet Robert Burns; musician Etta James; novelist Virginia Woolf

January 26 · Aquarius · You make your own rules and are not afraid to strike out in unexpected directions. Your strength of character and steely intelligence give you a unique persona. Because you know the value of power, you are unlikely to misuse it. You thrive under pressure and need to prove what you're made of.

AVOID: Unhappiness; unfocused energy; spite

ALSO BORN ON THIS DAY: Hockey star Wayne Gretzky; U.S. General Douglas MacArthur; actor Paul Newman

January 27 · **Aquarius** ·

People born on January 27 have excitable, magnetic personalities. You are alternately focused and indifferent. You may have trouble balancing the disparate sides of your nature, but this disparity is one of your most intriguing traits. You have a taste for exotic romance and may have trouble being faithful, because although your heart is true, your spirit wanders. You can relate to individuals of all backgrounds and temperaments. Your talent for perceiving the motives of others is extraordinary. Although you are not especially goal-oriented, you do set your sights on big dreams.

AVOID: Perplexity; hoping against hope; inertia

ALSO BORN ON THIS DAY: Dancer/actor Mikhail Baryshnikov; author Lewis Carroll; composer Wolfgang Amadeus Mozart

January 28 · **Aquarius** ·

You see yourself as a work in progress. You don't expect to assimilate all the experiences in your life overnight. While you hope for perfection, you realize it isn't likely and you have the common sense to be as tolerant and forgiving of your own faults as those of others. You are quite competitive, with an affinity for math, science, and music, and you have a talent for analytical reasoning. You aren't big on plans; you prefer to take life as it comes, no matter the consequences. You are curious about life, and that keeps you interested.

AVOID: Fears; chaos; dictatorial behavior

ALSO BORN ON THIS DAY: Artist Jackson Pollock; pianist Arthur Rubenstein; French President Nicolas Sarkozy

The Water Bearer

January 29 · **Aquarius** · You are not content to watch the parade go by—you are spurred on by a powerful sense of mission. Although you may appear somewhat prickly, you are actually gentle and philosophical in nature. You will put your reputation on the line to bring about necessary change. You have a talent for inspiring and influencing others. You are often afraid of commitment because it represents loss of independence. You want to help others see the power and beauty of life. You love and respect knowledge and wish to share it with others.

AVOID: Selfishness; controversy; destructive acts

ALSO BORN ON THIS DAY: Writer Anton Chekhov; feminist Germaine Greer; TV host Oprah Winfrey

January 30 · **Aquarius** · You have aristocratic bearing and leadership ability yet are extremely accessible and friendly. You are generous and somewhat self-deprecating. It may be difficult for you to see your good traits without having them validated by loved ones. Although you seem serious, you know how to have a good time. You need your emotional space and will not sacrifice your independence. Your goals are often too complicated for the average person to understand. In fact, you tend to be so unconcerned with conventional goals that you may achieve prominence because of your indifference.

AVOID: Lost opportunities; misjudging others; surliness

ALSO BORN ON THIS DAY: Actor Vanessa Redgrave; U.S. President Franklin D. Roosevelt; chess champion Boris Spassky

The Water Bearer

January 31 · Aquarius ·
You have an eccentric perspective, with the charisma to charm just about anyone. You are smart and talented, but your intelligence can be undermined by foolish choices. You have the ability to see beyond your concerns and look at life on a global level, and you'll always find time to help others.

AVOID: Addiction; immaturity; silliness

ALSO BORN ON THIS DAY: Novelist Norman Mailer; baseball star Jackie Robinson; composer Franz Schubert

February 1 · Aquarius ·
You are a rare breed: a rebel with respect for values. You can come too close to the dark side of your personality and must confront it. You have a desire to show your independence.

AVOID: Superstition; losing interest; disappointment

ALSO BORN ON THIS DAY: Actor Clark Gable; poet Langston Hughes; musician Rick James

February 2 · Aquarius ·
You are a stickler for honesty. You need to display your unconventional personality. Liberty and self-determination are your chief goals. You don't care what you have to do or what you have to give up, as long as it provides autonomy.

AVOID: Stifling your own creativity; bad habits; loose talk

ALSO BORN ON THIS DAY: Actor Farrah Fawcett; novelist James Joyce; novelist Ayn Rand

The Water Bearer

February 3 · Aquarius · People born on February 3 are

talented, modest, and charming. You see the big picture and life's small details. You can be eccentric, yet you may shelter yourself beneath a personality that reflects conventional views. You put faith in planning, knowing that hard work pays off. You are devoted to family life. You have a strong sense of humanitarianism and are happy to use your power to shift focus to those less fortunate. You have a strong conscience, which balances what may sometimes seem to be a narcissistic side.

AVOID: Emotional instability; pretense; self-interest

ALSO BORN ON THIS DAY: Composer Felix Mendelssohn; illustrator Norman Rockwell; poet Gertrude Stein

February 4 · Aquarius · The men and women born on this

date are intelligent and quirky; they can give the impression of being "airheads," but in reality they are more practical than they seem. You are inspired by what can be achieved through hard work. You have enormous self-discipline and can be extremely austere when it comes to cutting unnecessary encumbrances. Strong friendships are among the greatest joys in your life. If only half of the goals you envision come true, you will consider yourself fortunate. You often tilt at windmills, yet your deep commitment makes it impossible for you to behave any other way.

AVOID: A critical demeanor; public opinion; cruelty

ALSO BORN ON THIS DAY: Aviator Charles Lindbergh; activist Rosa Parks; football star Lawrence Taylor

The Water Bearer

February 5 · Aquarius · People born on this date are
intense and magnetic. Paradoxically, you also have a loner mentality
and introspective nature, though you can shine socially. You are
haughty yet lovable. You have a strict code of behavior and generally
have strong religious or spiritual beliefs. You have a thoroughly
modern outlook but are set in your ways. You place less importance
on your personal life than most people. Yet when you manage to
find a relationship that works, you are spiritually and emotionally
energized.

AVOID: Foolish risks; envy; codependency

ALSO BORN ON THIS DAY: Baseball star Hank Aaron; actor John
Carradine; football star Roger Staubach

February 6 · Aquarius · You possess a strong sense of
personal integrity and the ability to act as a mediator. You embrace
humanity and use your talents and personal goodness for the benefit
of others. You have so much charm that even rivals compliment
you. With a solid gift for friendship, you are eager to invite others
into your circle. You have the potential for greatness, though you
seldom realize this yourself. You are an ideologue and may find it
difficult to reconcile your beliefs with the practical methods needed
to make them reality. You have high ideals, and your primary goal is
to uphold them.

AVOID: Capitulation; self-interest; wasting resources

ALSO BORN ON THIS DAY: TV journalist Tom Brokaw; U.S.
President Ronald Reagan; baseball star Babe Ruth

February 7 · Aquarius · You are a private person, but your great personal charm makes you popular. You have a need to express your strong opinions. You are adventurous.

AVOID: Bitterness; emotional detachment; lies

ALSO BORN ON THIS DAY: Musician Garth Brooks; novelist Charles Dickens; comedian Chris Rock

~~~

February 8 · Aquarius · Friends play a special role in your life. Because your interests are generally philosophical, making a career choice can be difficult. The perfect freedom you seek does not exist. You must work hard to harness the discipline and energy to stay focused on professional tasks.

AVOID: Carelessness; lack of focus; indifference

ALSO BORN ON THIS DAY: Actor James Dean; TV journalist Ted Koppel; composer and conductor John Williams

~~~

February 9 · Aquarius · You possess a combination of innocence and wisdom. You feel a strong need to communicate your ideas through action. You accept struggle with grace, knowing you can become what you envision only through hard work. You go where your emotions take you. You work well in partnership. You are not content to wait for things to happen.

AVOID: Hostility; ill wishes; unpredictability

ALSO BORN ON THIS DAY: Actor Mia Farrow; musician Carole King; writer Alice Walker

~~~

The Water Bearer

February 10 · **Aquarius** · People born on this date are
high-energy types whose ambition for worldly success is grounded
in motives other than materialism. You believe in your abilities
but are not egocentric. You fight for the underdog and use your
own resources to help others. Your ability to see beyond your own
concerns is a praiseworthy characteristic. You have real concern and
love for others and are able to look at the total person without any
judgment or pettiness. You are generous with your money, but not
in a frivolous way. In your personal life, you seek to bridge the gap
between loneliness and a sense of peace and contentment.

AVOID: Mediocrity; worry; irresponsibility

ALSO BORN ON THIS DAY: Golf star Greg Norman; Olympian
Mark Spitz; actor Robert Wagner

February 11 · **Aquarius** · You understand the powerful
forces that can be commanded with discipline and training. You
have a single-mindedness that allows you to sacrifice to bring a goal
to fruition. Despite your seriousness, you have a sunny side. You're
able to balance all the elements in your life without losing focus or
emotional centeredness. In your opinion, no one can have too many
friends. Despite your reputation for enjoying the good life, you have
a domestic side. You are all about commitment and find it hard to
walk away from a challenge.

AVOID: Perfectionism; bad temper; exhaustion

ALSO BORN ON THIS DAY: Actor Jennifer Aniston; inventor
Thomas Edison; novelist Sidney Sheldon

The Water Bearer

February 12 · Aquarius · Men and women born on

February 12 have quiet strength. Your wisdom is based on karmic experience, yet you can live according to society's constraints. You have the spiritual power to heal others' psychic wounds. Your Aquarian nature draws people to you, but you are a loner at heart and may have a difficult time making close friends. You possess a haughty personality and enjoy showing off on the social scene. Smart use of your psychic awareness for practical applications in life is your chief goal. You are capable of spectacular things.

AVOID: Negativity; disinterest; failure

ALSO BORN ON THIS DAY: Naturalist Charles Darwin; U.S. President Abraham Lincoln; ballerina Anna Pavlova

February 13 · Aquarius · Overcoming odds is what you

live for, so you may invite a struggle when there's no need to do so! You have incredible energy, though you may not always use it wisely. You find it easy to get through life on your charm and good looks— but glitter is only one of your sides. You are good-hearted and fun-loving, and you don't expect a lot—only good companionship and an occasional shoulder to lean on. Your life goals may be unusual, but you can achieve them with determination and focus. You don't generally put all your ambition into career aims, preferring to indulge the personal side of life.

AVOID: Inattention to detail; insincerity; gloating

ALSO BORN ON THIS DAY: Actor Kim Novak; artist Grant Wood; pilot Chuck Yeager

The Water Bearer

February 14 · Aquarius ·

You possess an analytical intelligence that allows you to tackle complex problems without losing sight of the practical side issues. You have an edgy charm that makes you irresistible. Your optimism makes you believe that anything worthwhile can—and eventually will—happen.

AVOID: Mental exhaustion; prejudice; false hope

ALSO BORN ON THIS DAY: Journalist Carl Bernstein; New York City Mayor Michael Bloomberg; union president Jimmy Hoffa

February 15 · Aquarius ·

You exude sophistication, along with an aura of mystery and charm. You are the picture of romanticism. Your sarcasm is usually reserved for extreme situations, but most of your loved ones have felt its sting.

AVOID: Shallowness; frivolous emotion; excesses

ALSO BORN ON THIS DAY: Activist Susan B. Anthony; actor John Barrymore; cartoonist Matt Groening

February 16 · Aquarius ·

Easygoing and generous, you give freely of your time and talents. You have a laid-back attitude that endears you to everyone; however, you are a perfectionist. When you involve yourself in a project, you give it everything. You are dedicated to getting maximum excitement out of life.

AVOID: Quitting; discouragement; lost opportunities

ALSO BORN ON THIS DAY: Entertainer/politician Sonny Bono; actor LeVar Burton; tennis star John McEnroe

The Water Bearer

February 17 · **Aquarius** · You are stable and intense, with strong views, yet you prefer to express yourself nonverbally. You are precocious emotionally and intellectually, and you occasionally fear the intensity of your feelings, so you make it a point to keep your emotions in check. You give the impression of being strong and capable, yet there are times when you feel on edge. You want to succeed as you play by the rules, and it's important to you to maintain integrity in your personal relationships—the superficial trappings of purely social relationships mean little to you.

AVOID: Derision; dependence; losing faith

ALSO BORN ON THIS DAY: Comedian Larry the Cable Guy; actor Hal Holbrook; basketball star Michael Jordan

February 18 · **Aquarius** · You are dedicated to the art of perfection and look at every goal as a personal challenge. You can transcend the mundane trivia of everyday life to become something special. You not only attract controversy—you thrive on it! You are quiet and introspective, and you have what it takes to be emotionally self-sufficient. When challenges come your way, you bear up stoically. You're tough on yourself, always looking to make each challenge more meaningful than the one that came before. You have good taste and like living well, but you would never subvert your beliefs in order to make a good salary.

AVOID: Making demands; psychological strain; irritability

ALSO BORN ON THIS DAY: Filmmaker John Hughes; novelist Toni Morrison; actor Molly Ringwald

The Fish

February 19 · Pisces · You have incredibly high ideals and
are eager to learn, to discover. You are restless, eccentrically spiritual,
and lean toward being emotionally fragile. At times, you are unable
to assert your authority and thus have to struggle not to be managed
by others. Governed by your emotions, you can sometimes be your
own worst enemy. You are charming, kindhearted, and generous,
but you tend to have a hard time feeling good about yourself; instead
you rely on validation from friends and lovers. You are devoted to
your dreams. Because of your selfless nature, many of your dreams
are for others.

AVOID: Predictability; censure; irresponsibility

ALSO BORN ON THIS DAY: Astronomer Nicolas Copernicus;
musician Smokey Robinson; writer Amy Tan

February 20 · Pisces · Men and women born on this date
are deeply attuned to the spiritual mysteries of life. You possess
a phenomenal memory. Your considerable intelligence tends to
be more of an esoteric understanding than an analytical skill.
You have high ideals, though you aren't necessarily a practical
creature. Your lack of self-confidence leads you to choose unworthy
companions. In your romantic life, you must learn to value rational
love over obsessive love. Learn how to set limits in your personal
relationships, and you'll be considerably calmer.

AVOID: Doubts; pretense; sleep disruption

ALSO BORN ON THIS DAY: Photographer Ansel Adams; actor
Sidney Poitier; fashion designer Gloria Vanderbilt

The Fish

February 21 · **Pisces** · You are acquisitive without being
materialistic. You seek prestige but are generous with resources.
Those close to you know they can always come to you for help. You
are fun-loving, yet you also embrace responsibility.

Avoid: Intrigue; spendthrift habits; tension

Also born on this day: Writer Erma Bombeck; entertainment
mogul David Geffen; musician Nina Simone

February 22 · **Pisces** · You have great courage and are
always ready to make tough decisions. More than anything else, you
want to be allowed to live your life in a way you find pleasing. You
are merely being true to your own instincts when you ignore the fast
lane and choose to go through life at your own pace.

Avoid: Betrayal; confusion; disillusionment

Also born on this day: Composer Frederic Chopin; poet Edna
St. Vincent Millay; U.S. President George Washington

February 23 · **Pisces** · You have the ability to reach
emotional fulfillment on many levels and are not limited to the more
orthodox understanding of spirituality that sustains others. You
discover reality through a heightened sensitivity that can be difficult
for all but those closest to you to understand.

Avoid: Self-pity; intolerant people; striking an attitude

Also born on this day: Writer W. E. B. DuBois; actor Peter
Fonda; composer George Frideric Handel

The Fish

February 24 · Pisces · You have a natural dynamism that
sets you apart from other Pisceans. You are a go-getter who enjoys
a varied and interesting social life. You may have difficulty finding
a focus in your life, but when you do, you are true to it. You are
drawn to the humanitarian professions: counseling, health care, or
child care. Empathetic rather than just sympathetic, you have the
ability to understand the pain of others. You are extremely romantic.
No matter how often your heart is broken, you have the ability to
bounce back. You are far more concerned with looking forward than
wondering what might have been.

AVOID: Resistance; formality; pride

ALSO BORN ON THIS DAY: Apple founder Steve Jobs; composer
Michel Legrand; actor Edward James Olmos

February 25 · Pisces · You are in tune with the world
around you. You are ruled by instinct and intuition, yet you
appreciate the value of an intellectual point of view. You have the
potential to do great things, but you are even more powerful when
you put your talents toward a cause greater than yourself. You have
an instinct for understanding and empathizing with the problems
and concerns of others. Because your goals often change with your
moods, you are on a constant search for new challenges and new
horizons.

AVOID: Instability; conceit; distractions

ALSO BORN ON THIS DAY: Musician George Harrison; actor
Rashida Jones; artist Pierre August Renoir

The Fish

February 26 · Pisces · You see life on a large scale, yet your ability to perceive details is nothing short of amazing. You are affectionate and gentle, and although your ambition to succeed is very strong, you never lose sight of the importance of personal relationships. You extract the maximum from experience and never regret an opportunity taken, even if it doesn't bring you the happiness you expected. You are extremely idealistic in your hopes and perceptions. You see no reason why your dreams can't be realized and are willing to sacrifice to make sure that they are.

AVOID: Egotism; unpredictability; anger

ALSO BORN ON THIS DAY: Musician Johnny Cash; comedian Jackie Gleason; novelist Victor Hugo

February 27 · Pisces · You have great empathy for others. You are especially protective of those you love and will go to any lengths to secure their happiness. Your intelligence shows in the application of your intuitive talents. You are skilled at managing the lives of others and often take charge of situations outside of your circle. You have the ability to shine at almost anything you attempt, and you often turn your talents toward helping others. You are fearless when it comes to stating your opinions on the most controversial matters, and you have the power to effect great change and understanding.

AVOID: Flightiness; insecurity; jealous rages

ALSO BORN ON THIS DAY: Musician Marian Anderson; dancer Antoinette Sibley; novelist John Steinbeck

The Fish

February 28 · **Pisces** · It is typical for people with this
birthday to strive for perfection. You dream on such a lofty scale
that your reach at times exceeds your grasp. You enjoy living in the
limelight and gravitate toward a fast-paced lifestyle.

AVOID: Excesses; no-win situations; enemies

ALSO BORN ON THIS DAY: Race car driver Mario Andretti; filmmaker Vincente Minnelli; actor Bernadette Peters

February 29 · **Pisces** · Owing to your unusual birth date,
you have unique talents and characteristics. You are good-natured,
friendly, and almost unbelievably optimistic. You have a brilliant
talent for seeing the positive side of any issue, and while you are not
naive, you do retain a measure of your childhood innocence.

AVOID: Trying too hard; childishness; making demands

ALSO BORN ON THIS DAY: Motivational speaker Tony Robbins;
composer Gioacchino Rossini; musician Dinah Shore

March 1 · **Pisces** · You have strong views on morality, and
your need to understand your own motivations is very strong. You
respect the status quo but rarely seek to live your life in search of it.
You are highly competitive and give your best at every opportunity,
always believing that attitude, more than ability, promises success.

AVOID: Charlatans; emotional instability; needless worry

ALSO BORN ON THIS DAY: Musician Harry Belafonte; actor/
filmmaker Ron Howard; bandleader Glenn Miller

The Fish

March 2 · Pisces · People born on March 2 have a perception

that borders on genius. Although you may seem to clear everything through intellectual channels, you are really exercising your psychic sensitivity. Most of your major life decisions are made in this way. You are a gentle soul who may lack self-confidence. This is unfortunate, because you have many talents and can actually "find" yourself through judicious application of your abilities. You have a great need to display your intellect through practical means. You work very hard to make your dreams a reality.

AVOID: Insecure friends; dilemmas; scheming

ALSO BORN ON THIS DAY: Writer Theodor Geisel (Dr. Seuss); Russian statesman Mikhail Gorbachev; novelist John Irving

March 3 · Pisces · Men and women born on this date have

an air of glamour about them. Although you often approach life from a dreamer's perspective, at the same time, you tend to be fairly aggressive and opinionated. Professional goals are a definite priority, and success is an important goal in your life, although you have a natural reluctance to ask others for help. When you connect with someone in a meaningful friendship, however, the relationship is likely to last for a lifetime. For you to achieve your goals, you must accept challenges. You are also tuned in to life's spiritual aspects and may be drawn to the supernatural.

AVOID: Passivity; fear of commitment; personal obsessions

ALSO BORN ON THIS DAY: Inventor Alexander Graham Bell; designer Perry Ellis; Olympian Jackie Joyner-Kersee

The Fish

March 4 • Pisces •
At times, life may seem to be a battlefield to the courageous and iconoclastic people born on this date. You attract upheaval and chaos, creating a never-ending cycle of change. You have a great deal of nervous energy and are rarely comfortable in sedentary jobs. You hold yourself to a very rigid code of conduct, testing your character at every turn, and you have an all-or-nothing mentality. If you cannot reach the highest goals you have set for yourself, you may not be interested in attempting anything on a more modest scale. The challenge that awaits you is to work toward your lofty ambitions while also pursuing reachable goals.

AVOID: Going to extremes; deliberation; blaming others

ALSO BORN ON THIS DAY: Football coach Knute Rockne; composer Antonio Vivaldi; musician Bobby Womack

March 5 • Pisces •
People born on March 5 possess considerable intellectual courage. You are rarely afraid to take a stand or to own up to your controversial opinions. Even if you face stiff opposition to your ideas or plans, you will not allow dissent from others to sway you from your course. You are talkative and friendly, and you have a talent for using words to your own benefit. You put a great price on the opportunity to share ideas and feelings with those close to you. You attract conflict and enjoy the chance to overcome it through your own efforts and hard work.

AVOID: Ego issues; wildness; arguments

ALSO BORN ON THIS DAY: Playwright Charles Fuller; actor Rex Harrison; composer Heitor Villa-Lobos

The Fish

March 6 · **Pisces** · You are a free spirit who refuses to conform to ordinary standards. You are not rebellious, since you respect structure, yet you choose to live outside it. You are unafraid to take chances and would rather fail grandly than be too timid to try. You are unique in the extreme.

AVOID: Snobbishness; empty promises; fatalism

ALSO BORN ON THIS DAY: Poet Elizabeth Barrett Browning; basketball star Shaquille O'Neal; filmmaker Rob Reiner

March 7 · **Pisces** · March 7 individuals are very creative. These dreamy souls are true visionaries. You are empathetic. Your sensitivity can transcend relationships of all types and definition. Highly evolved in every way, you are accountable only to yourself.

AVOID: Rage; confusion; feelings of inferiority

ALSO BORN ON THIS DAY: Football star Franco Harris; composer Maurice Ravel; actor Rachel Weisz

March 8 · **Pisces** · You are puzzling and provocative, a fascinating combination of cynic and mystic. You may possess a loner mentality, yet you love people. You have a deep psychic consciousness, and you may prefer to spend your time pursuing humanitarian aims in a worldly forum.

AVOID: Fear; compromise; an unforgiving nature

ALSO BORN ON THIS DAY: Dancer Cyd Charisse; actor Aidan Quinn; actor Lynn Redgrave

The Fish

March 9 · Pisces · You are devoted to the pursuit of
excellence in all endeavors. You are extraordinarily sensitive at the
core, yet are outwardly strong and determined. You are genuine and
truthful. You have a great regard for spirituality in all its aspects
and also possess a wicked sense of humor that infects even your
most serious moments. You have very little regard for artifice and
will freely speak out against it. You treasure your friends and allow
them the sort of emotional intimacy most people reserve only for
mates and family members. You are constantly perusing your own
character, searching for the one reality that will explore and explain
the totality of your existence.

AVOID: Caution; pretense; superstition

ALSO BORN ON THIS DAY: Chess champion Bobby Fischer;
cosmonaut Yuri Gagarin; writer Mickey Spillane

March 10 · Pisces · You know how to draw the spotlight
in any situation, and you usually manage to keep it on yourself for
as long as you choose. Although you display a flirty, semiserious
personality, there's considerable grit beneath the surface of your
good humor. You can take care of yourself on just about any level
and will never let anyone get the better of you. You have a great
respect for learning and a reverence for wisdom, and you are
dedicated to passing your knowledge to others. You believe in
working to positively affect the next generation.

AVOID: Inflexibility; an implacable nature; coldness

ALSO BORN ON THIS DAY: Actor/martial arts star Chuck Norris;
abolitionist Harriet Tubman; musician Carrie Underwood

The Fish

March 11 · **Pisces** · You have the temperament of a true
artisan. You are a gentle yet determined soul, and you follow a very
personal path throughout life. You are drawn to extremes and are a
stickler for truth. You are committed to finding inner peace.

Avoid: Distractions; pettiness; worry

Also born on this day: Writer Douglas Adams; musician
Bobby McFerrin; bandleader Lawrence Welk

March 12 · **Pisces** · You bring creativity and grace to
everything you do. You are fantasy-oriented, and you possess a
spiritually centered type of intelligence. You are incapable of acting
from a strictly selfish perspective and are usually willing to sacrifice
your own interests to accommodate those you love.

Avoid: Destructive impulses; confusion; guilt

Also born on this day: Actor Liza Minnelli; dancer/
choreographer Vaslav Nijinsky; musician James Taylor

March 13 · **Pisces** · People with this birthday have a
reputation for being high-strung. You find it difficult to "go with the
flow." Although generous by nature, at times you may have trouble
accommodating the views and needs of others. You have a strong
sense of self and seldom question your own judgment.

Avoid: Resentments; mistrust; meddling

Also born on this day: Astronaut Gene Cernan; actor William
H. Macy; musician Neil Sedaka

The Fish

March 14 · Pisces · You combine intelligence with profound
creative insight. Prophetic and poetic, you seem at times to be on
another plane of existence. You don't make friends easily, but once
you do, it's for keeps. You must feel needed and indispensable or
you cannot give of yourself. You have an artistic sensibility that is
incredibly rewarding to yourself and others. Whatever you choose
to do in life, that creative perspective will make itself felt. You rarely
strive for success in any dollar-oriented way, yet you are likely to set
personal goals that act as signposts on your journey through life.

AVOID: Naïveté; impulsiveness; the blues

ALSO BORN ON THIS DAY: Physicist Albert Einstein; musician
Quincy Jones; composer Johann Strauss Sr.

March 15 · Pisces · You are as straightforward as they come.
You take things at face value and tend to be idealistic in all aspects
of life, often refusing to address the questionable motives of others.
Despite your intelligence, there is a certain naïveté about you, which
instantly endears you to others. You really cannot comprehend
selfish behavior and are put off by negativity of any kind. You are
sincere about your friendships, and you put your emotional and
psychic energy at the disposal of those you love. Career stress can get
to you, but you blow off steam through laughter. You wish to live a
life that's simple and meaningful, honest and productive.

AVOID: Cynicism; emotional obsession; unreality

ALSO BORN ON THIS DAY: Filmmaker David Cronenberg; actor
Judd Hirsch; U.S. President Andrew Jackson

The Fish

March 16 · Pisces · You have a high-stakes attitude toward
life. You are idealistic, yet have a wonderful capacity to understand
and empathize with the struggles of others. You are a great
cheerleader for your friends—you're unfailingly interested in their
lives, and you do what you can to participate. It's important for you
to find a harmonious balance between your career and personal
life. You require a sense of security in your life. Learning to trust in
the future can be a major breakthrough for you, as it eliminates the
stresses that do so much damage to your peace of mind.

AVOID: Compromise; being controlled; sexual excesses

ALSO BORN ON THIS DAY: Filmmaker Bernardo Bertolucci; actor
Isabelle Huppert; U.S. President James Madison

March 17 · Pisces · There is a hard edge of reality to you,
even though you are warmly sensitive to your environment and
day-to-day situations. You have the ability to set aside your creative
endeavors and address practical problems when necessary. Nothing
is a hurdle to you because you have an innate sense of what should
take priority at any given time. Career goals are likely to be a
major force through which all other aspirations are filtered. You
are concerned with bringing together your dreamy side and your
practical side. You vacillate between being an incurable romantic
and a hard-boiled cynic.

AVOID: Defensiveness; fatalism; wasting resources

ALSO BORN ON THIS DAY: Musician Nat King Cole; golf star
Bobby Jones; actor Gary Sinise

The Fish

March 18 · Pisces · You depend upon your strong psychic awareness to guide your actions. You sometimes may appear to be caught up in compulsive—even reckless—behavior. However, you are actually very centered. You are on a continual search for adventure. You embrace challenges.

Avoid: Trade-offs; psychic pain; loss

Also born on this day: Olympian Bonnie Blair; writer George Plimpton; novelist John Updike

March 19 · Pisces · You are sensitive and possess a sunny disposition. Although you can easily give yourself over to intuition, you understand the need to ground yourself in common sense. You are goal-oriented. You are also charming in an unassuming way.

Avoid: Restrictions; disparity; turbulence

Also born on this day: Novelist Philip Roth; Supreme Court Justice Earl Warren; actor Bruce Willis

March 20 · Pisces · You draw a veil between others and your real self. You are naturally drawn to the past, whether as a fount of your unconscious desires or the pool of your conflicted memories. You must learn to manage the impulses of your own creative psyche.

Avoid: Controversy; regret; suspicion

Also born on this day: Playwright Henrik Ibsen; filmmaker Spike Lee; hockey star Bobby Orr

The Ram

March 21 · Aries ·
You have a proud, adventuresome, energetic nature, though this may not be displayed in conventional ways. You are sure of yourself and your convictions, but you may fear being ridiculed for your great dreams. For this reason you are likely to adopt a "who cares" attitude, when in truth you care very much. You have incredible emotional resilience and can easily bounce back from disappointment. You have a quiet intensity that is riveting. Although you do not make a great display of yourself, you draw others to you easily. Positions of power come naturally to March 21 individuals, whether in the business or academic arenas.

AVOID: Superstition; indolence; becoming too cautious

ALSO BORN ON THIS DAY: Composer Johann Sebastian Bach; poet Phyllis McGinley; theatrical producer Florenz Ziegfeld

March 22 · Aries ·
Instinct takes precedence over intellect in your life. You are impulsive and fun-loving and enjoy testing boundaries and breaking the rules. You are vibrant and exciting and can draw people to you on the strength of your personality alone. You are a natural leader, but not in the conventional sense. Others envy your love of daring and risk-taking. You have the highest expectations for your own success and may be unable to recognize the pitfalls that are possible when striving hard to reach a goal. A strong belief in yourself is a key factor in your overall success.

AVOID: Personal obsessions; needless worry; bad habits

ALSO BORN ON THIS DAY: Mime Marcel Marceau; composer/lyricist Stephen Sondheim; composer/producer Andrew Lloyd Webber

The Ram

March 23 · **Aries** · People born on this date are self-deprecating, good-natured folks who typically don't take themselves too seriously. You approach life with gusto and are never at a loss to find new and interesting subjects to engage your intellect. You have a quick mind and are able to store facts on many subjects for use at later times. Talkative and outgoing, you give the appearance of being highly organized, though you actually prefer to take life as it comes, favoring spontaneity over any carefully orchestrated plan to succeed. You have high expectations but leave it up to providence to make your dreams come true.

AVOID: Excessive temperament; ignoring details; intolerance

ALSO BORN ON THIS DAY: Musician Damon Albarn; actor Joan Crawford; filmmaker Akira Kurosawa

March 24 · **Aries** · You are a creative, sympathetic type and see your life as an expression of your deep inner creativity. Your good nature extends to associations with everyone around you, and you are unlikely to have enemies. You possess a delightful naïveté that in no way implies a lack of intelligence or sophistication. You manage to combine these qualities with a simplicity that attracts admirers. You have a general idea of what you want to happen in your life, but it is likely to be tempered by your wonder and enjoyment at watching events unfold in your own time.

AVOID: Losing momentum; codependency; negative thoughts

ALSO BORN ON THIS DAY: Actor Robert Carradine; fashion designer Bob Mackie; actor Steve McQueen

The Ram

March 25 · Aries · Your inner nature is very different from
your outer personality. You are often the life of the party, but in truth
you are naturally shy, preferring your own company to crowds. You
draw strength from a rich and creative inner life.

AVOID: Pessimism; looking back instead of forward; being sullen

ALSO BORN ON THIS DAY: Musician Aretha Franklin; musician
Elton John; author/activist Gloria Steinem

March 26 · Aries · On the surface you appear to be
unflappable, yet there is an insecurity at your core that can create
emotional distress. You are unlikely to show your vulnerabilities to
the world. You prefer to handle your own challenges, solve your own
problems. You believe in your own ability to make things happen.

AVOID: Being secretive; ignoring the needs of others; sarcasm

ALSO BORN ON THIS DAY: Supreme Court Justice Sandra Day
O'Connor; musician Diana Ross; playwright Tennessee Williams

March 27 · Aries · Strength and tenacity are your defining
characteristics. You generally go your own way and make your
decisions according to your impulsive nature. You dream big dreams
and expect them to come true. You work amazingly hard to achieve
these ends.

AVOID: Insincerity; becoming disillusioned; trying too hard

ALSO BORN ON THIS DAY: Musician Mariah Carey; actor Gloria
Swanson; filmmaker Quentin Tarantino

The Ram

March 28 · Aries · You have a bubbly, excitable, and
somewhat unpredictable personality. You can be argumentative, but
never to the point where it diminishes your great personal charm. At
your core you are thoughtful, meditative, and spiritual. You spend
a great deal of time and effort balancing these conflicting qualities.
Even when you don't have a specific goal in mind, you are on a
constant pilgrimage to improve your life. You invariably draw others
into this personal commitment to excellence, inspiring you in ways
no one else could.

AVOID: Putting yourself first; demanding perfection; being petty

ALSO BORN ON THIS DAY: Musician Lady Gaga; Renaissance
artist Raphael (Raffaello Santi); actor Vince Vaughn

March 29 · Aries · There is a poetic quality to the people
born on this day, a sense of combining the insubstantial with the
ethereal. You have the ability to transcend the ordinary aspects of
your personality by drawing upon a penetrating intelligence and
extraordinary gifts of intuition. You do not always realize you are
making a determination by instinct rather than intelligence. You
are extra sensitive to the thoughts and projections of others and are
incredibly connected to the people in your life. Friendship has a
special meaning for you, and you wisely choose friends who are as
different from yourself as possible.

AVOID: Envy; wishing others ill; wasting time

ALSO BORN ON THIS DAY: Musician Pearl Bailey; comedian Eric
Idle; baseball legend Cy Young

The Ram

March 30 · Aries · You are renowned for your sense of
humor. Bold and generous, you live life to the fullest and are seldom
afraid to take chances on your self-appointed path to wisdom and
enlightenment. You are an enthusiastic and dynamic individual with
the ability to spur others to action. You make a fine mentor and will
go to any lengths to help friends and associates attain their goals.
You know what you want out of life. Even though you may end up
taking a rather circuitous route to get where you are going, you
understand that sometimes the journey is more enlightening than
the final destination.

AVOID: Hurtful criticism; superficial friendships; conflict

ALSO BORN ON THIS DAY: Actor Warren Beatty; musician Eric
Clapton; artist Vincent van Gogh

March 31 · Aries · Your uniqueness owes itself in part to your
ability to recognize unusual opportunities. You often seem to be
in the path of miraculous good fortune, but it is to your credit that
when such a rendezvous takes place, you know how to benefit from
it. You have a great deal of charisma and can make things happen by
the strength and force of your personality alone. You are ambitious
about making your dreams become reality. You don't hold yourself
to set standards, preferring to chart your own course. Far from being
concerned with your own success, you like to feel that your choices
influence and even benefit humankind as a whole.

AVOID: Senseless unpredictability; being late; self-doubt

ALSO BORN ON THIS DAY: Activist César Chávez; designer Liz
Claiborne; philosopher René Descartes

The Ram

April 1 · Aries ·

Despite your connection to this "holiday," you are anything but a fool. You are a leader, though not in the conventional sense of that word. Your quiet nature masks an ability to make the best of any situation, no matter how challenging or unpleasant it may be. Although you are frequently centered on your own concerns (the way most Arians are), you rarely ignore an opportunity to help or inspire others. You have a magnetic charisma. You don't mind the ups and downs of life because you prefer to be caught up in extremes rather than dull routine.

AVOID: Insincerity; impractical hope; valuing only what you can see

ALSO BORN ON THIS DAY: Political commentator Rachel Maddow; composer Sergei Rachmaninoff; actor Debbie Reynolds

April 2 · Aries ·

You walk a fine line between what you know of life and what you wish to be true. You possess uncanny powers of imagination and may spend a great deal of your life dreaming with eyes wide open. You have a natural dignity that may cause you to seem standoffish to those who do not know you well. This reticence has a lordly resonance and creates an aura of specialness around you. You have confidence in your own ability to succeed and are slow to believe that anything happens merely by chance. Carefully planned moves and strategies helps you to achieve your life plans, and you will adhere stringently to those plans at any cost.

AVOID: Predictability; jealousy; boredom

ALSO BORN ON THIS DAY: Writer Hans Christian Andersen; musician Marvin Gaye; actor Alec Guinness

The Ram

April 3 · **Aries** · You see yourself as a citizen of the world. Although you may like to think of yourself as a social rebel, the truth is something quite different. You have great ambition, and almost a sixth sense about making the right choice at the right time.

Avoid: Coldheartedness; envy; empty praise

Also born on this day: Actor Marlon Brando; actor Doris Day; naturalist Jane Goodall

April 4 · **Aries** · You are marked by a quiet strength, and you possess the enviable talent of being able to be worldly and spiritual in equal measure. You inspire through example, yet you never seek to force others into your way of thinking. You make your greatest strides when the deck is stacked against you.

Avoid: Hurting others' feelings; arbitration; empty calories

Also born on this day: Poet Maya Angelou; composer Elmer Bernstein; actor/screenwriter Anthony Perkins

April 5 · **Aries** · Those born on April 5 are the natural aristocrats among people. You have a high opinion of yourself and may even be self-centered, although that attitude in no way influences your ability to interact with others or to be likable. Your best trait is unabashed honesty.

Avoid: Self-pity; capriciousness; overthinking

Also born on this day: Actor Bette Davis; actor Gregory Peck; U.S. Secretary of State Colin Powell

The Ram

April 6 • Aries •

Creativity and imagination of the highest level characterize those born on April 6. You are enormously talented and will use that talent as a means of expressing your life energy. An element of illusion runs through your life like a radiant thread. You have the ability to convince others of your opinions and aims, yet the manner in which you accomplish this is subtle and generally displayed rather than uttered. You have true "star quality." You have faith that the good you do will be returned to you, and for this reason you make it your business to promote a positive attitude in all areas of life.

AVOID: Constant worry; superficial relationships; gossip

ALSO BORN ON THIS DAY: Illusionist Harry Houdini; composer/conductor Andre Previn; actor Billy Dee Williams

April 7 • Aries •

You are a fascinating combination of dreamer and doer, and you will always put your talents to work in improving the conditions of those around you. You have the ability to sense other people's feelings and can become involved in others' problems and concerns while withholding judgment. Your dreams and goals, like most facets of your life, are played out on a huge scale with drama to spare. Although practicality is not usually one of your strengths, you can put this skill to work if your desire to succeed is great enough.

AVOID: Empty promises; selling yourself short; fatalism

ALSO BORN ON THIS DAY: Filmmaker Francis Ford Coppola; musician Billie Holiday; poet William Wordsworth

The Ram

April 8 · **Aries** · Despite a pleasing personality, you have steel
at your core and never miss a chance to learn from your mistakes.
You may be regarded as a potential mover and shaker, though your
interests are often on a more limited scale. You don't see yourself
as a catalyst for change but will endeavor to right a wrong if an
opportunity presents itself. Your moral and spiritual sturdiness is
a positive factor as you strive to achieve your dreams. No one can
convince you that a goal is unreachable—even if you face enormous
challenges, you do not give up and you do not complain.

AVOID: Promiscuity; insensitivity; burning bridges

ALSO BORN ON THIS DAY: Diplomat Kofi Annan; First Lady Betty
Ford; actor Mary Pickford

April 9 · **Aries** · Feisty and opinionated, you see life as a series
of missions, some of which are successful, some of which fail. More
pragmatic than idealistic, you enjoy striving almost as much as you
enjoy the victories your efforts bring. Your intrepid nature makes
you a virtual pioneer who is not afraid to challenge the status quo.
You know what you want out of life and aren't afraid to go after it.
You are intensely loyal and will always stand by a friend, especially
one who is in trouble. You may not settle on a career until you have
tried a great many options. You are unruffled by difficulty and see
setbacks as mere inconveniences.

AVOID: Looking back; saying "I told you so"; blaming others

ALSO BORN ON THIS DAY: Poet Charles Baudelaire; musician
Carl Perkins; actor Dennis Quaid

The Ram

April 10 · Aries · You're a fighter, though your sunny
personality may obscure this fact. You have your own way of doing
things. Though you manage to accomplish your aims in the nicest
possible way, there is never any doubt about how ambitious you
are. You have the capacity to see the world around you realistically,
without letting that knowledge cause disillusionment. You truly adore
people and consider your experiences with loved ones to be among
the cherished moments of your life. When good things happen to
you, you feel obligated to bestow good fortune on someone else.

AVOID: Manipulative people; indiscretions; giving in too easily

ALSO BORN ON THIS DAY: Ambassador/writer Clare Boothe
Luce; publisher/journalist Joseph Pulitzer; actor Omar Sharif

April 11 · Aries · Good-hearted and daring, people born on
this date have the potential to do a great deal of good in the world.
Whether you seek the broad arena of political activism or confine
your involvement to your proverbial own backyard, you display
the care and compassion that is too often missing from human
endeavors. You like to surround yourself with equals—partners who
share your sense of commitment to your own goals and causes. You
believe in your own ability to change the world. Even if specific goals
go unfulfilled, you know how to turn a negative experience into a
lesson learned.

AVOID: Seeking approval; focusing on weakness; controversy

ALSO BORN ON THIS DAY: Designer Oleg Cassini; musician Joss
Stone; poet Mark Strand

The Ram

April 12 · Aries · Armed with considerable intelligence,
curiosity, and drive, you are in a class by yourself. You are a
philosophical type who prizes learning, yet you don't confuse it
with wisdom. You are a student of the human condition and a keen
observer who can easily spot deception. You seek joy and positivity
in your relationships and will quickly leave any association that
promotes dependency or misunderstanding. Your ability to laugh
at yourself is refreshing. When you set your sights on a goal and
commit to it, you possess the will and ambition to make it a reality.

AVOID: Buying on credit; placing blame; seeing life from a single
point of view

ALSO BORN ON THIS DAY: Writer Beverly Cleary; musician
Herbie Hancock; TV host David Letterman

April 13 · Aries · There is definitely a spark of genius in people
born on April 13. These are not showy individuals, but people who
prefer existence in a humble—even obscure—setting. Although
you would never seek fame, it sometimes finds you. When it does,
it acts as a profound disruption in your life. You consider yourself
at the service of others, but your analytic characteristics can make
you seem rather cold. You go after what you want. Success and
achievement may be rather abstract terms to you, but you realize
that life is a game with many rules.

AVOID: Family disputes; being a people-pleaser; arrogance

ALSO BORN ON THIS DAY: Playwright Samuel Beckett; musician
Al Green; U.S. President Thomas Jefferson

The Ram

April 14 • **Aries** • Your great desire is to be happy and at peace. You are emphatically intelligent and are rarely afraid to question, to search, to dream. You are capable of doing great things, yet the significance to you isn't in the act, but in how you can translate the experience into an illuminating life lesson.

AVOID: Being too serious; antagonism; brooding

ALSO BORN ON THIS DAY: Actor Julie Christie; musician Loretta Lynn; baseball star Pete Rose

April 15 • **Aries** • Gifted and intuitive, you gain inspiration from the natural world. Even though you have a tendency to accumulate material possessions, you are far more in tune with the meaningful aspects of life. You aspire to be loved and rely upon the acceptance of those who are dear to you.

AVOID: Bragging; self-absorption; indecision

ALSO BORN ON THIS DAY: Artist Leonardo da Vinci; novelist Henry James; actor/screenwriter Emma Thompson

April 16 • **Aries** • You yearn to shine in the spotlight, even if only on a small scale. You have an agenda and aren't afraid to advertise it. You want to reach the top and will work very hard to get there. This applies to your spiritual journey as well as material goals.

AVOID: Needing to win; passing the buck; jumping to conclusions

ALSO BORN ON THIS DAY: Filmmaker/comedian Charlie Chaplin; composer Henry Mancini; musician Dusty Springfield

The Ram

April 17 · Aries ·

You seem to have an innate understanding of the world around you and all of its intricacies, and you are always ready to seize an opportunity. When you state an opinion, everyone in your circle is certain to view it as wisdom. From an early age you display a marked ability for leadership and tend to select like-minded friends. Your goals and expectations are in line with your abilities. You are a hard worker, dedicated to carrying out your responsibilities as best you can. Failure and setbacks only make you more determined to succeed.

AVOID: Guilt; self-criticism; danger

ALSO BORN ON THIS DAY: Actor William Holden; financier J. P. Morgan; playwright Thornton Wilder

April 18 · Aries ·

You are an eminent doer and achiever. When you set yourself a task, you will go to all lengths to accomplish it. Opinionated and aggressive, you often find yourself at the center of controversy. As long as there are causes to espouse and victories to be won, you are not the type to sit idly by. The enthusiasm with which you conduct your life draws others to you. Your goal is to open the eyes of those around you and create change. Because of their ability to inspire others, individuals born on April 18 make exceptional teachers, entrepreneurs, and politicians. In the rare event of a setback, you shrug off disappointment and begin again.

AVOID: Anger; hiding from the truth; attacking the motives of others

ALSO BORN ON THIS DAY: Attorney Clarence Darrow; composer Miklos Rozsa; artist Max Weber

The Ram

April 19 · Aries · You possess a deep sense of your own
spiritual significance and have the ability to do great things. You are
not interested in making a public show of your very personal aims,
yet the zeal that characterizes your ambition often gains you notice.
Although you are not a great planner, you do have a natural instinct
about what choices to make and when to make them. The decisions
you make may seem curious to others, but you rarely question
your intuition. You have a way of channeling your experiences and
relationships into spiritual and intellectual growth.

AVOID: Procrastination; disorganization; easily accepting failure

ALSO BORN ON THIS DAY: Actor Jayne Mansfield; FBI crime-
fighter Eliot Ness; designer Paloma Picasso

April 20 · Aries · You are guided by your emotions. Even
when you appear to make decisions based on logic and intellect,
you are actually tapping into the rich pipeline of your subconscious
mind. Because of your rich inner life, you sometimes appear to
live in a dream world. Although naturally contemplative, you can
summon the social élan needed to shine when the occasion arises.
You have a tendency to project your own needs and perceptions
onto the personalities of the people you love. Family is a strong force
in your life. Involvement in socially significant projects gives you a
sense of helping to make the world a better place.

AVOID: Being overly serious; distractions; making enemies

ALSO BORN ON THIS DAY: Actor Jessica Lange; artist Joan Miró;
Supreme Court Justice John Paul Stevens

The Bull

April 21 · **Taurus** · Your dynamism and sociability make you special. You have an interesting, spirited personality that attracts admirers in both your personal and professional life. You are extremely opinionated and at times have a problem accepting other points of view. Although your buoyant nature generally keeps you from seeming dogmatic or pushy, it is important that you cultivate tolerance on as broad a scale as you can muster. You are incredibly sentimental and romantic and believe that love was meant to last a lifetime. You believe in careful planning and are painstaking in your methods of bringing goals to fruition. You rarely let an opportunity go unfulfilled.

AVOID: Fearing change; ignoring lessons; going for broke

ALSO BORN ON THIS DAY: Novelist Charlotte Brontë; Russian empress Catherine the Great; Queen Elizabeth II of Great Britain

April 22 · **Taurus** · There is a certain level of instability inherent in your character and personality, which makes you appealing and attractive in an offbeat way. Unusual circumstances and coincidences are the spice of life for you, and you may unconsciously draw excitement and danger into your life. Quirky and unconventional, you take life as it comes. The idea of plotting a course for success seems alien, even foolish, to you. You trust in your own ability to make choices that will bring you the satisfaction and fulfillment you want, as well as provide the excitement you need.

AVOID: Fear; interrupting; careless mistakes

ALSO BORN ON THIS DAY: Philosopher Immanuel Kant; actor Jack Nicholson; filmmaker John Waters

The Bull

April 23 · **Taurus** · You have a brilliant and original mind. Your opinions generally run counter to conventional wisdom, and you don't care who disagrees with you. You are a joyous, irrepressible individual with the gift for making other people happy.

AVOID: Dishonest reasoning; irreverence; selfishness

ALSO BORN ON THIS DAY: Novelist Vladimir Nabokov; musician Roy Orbison; playwright William Shakespeare

April 24 · **Taurus** · People born on April 24 have a flair for the good life and a love of glamour. You are a practical person who plays by the rules. You are also talented, with a good sense of humor and the ability to laugh at yourself. You have big dreams and the determination to mold those dreams into reality.

AVOID: Getting even; feeling unappreciated; making excuses

ALSO BORN ON THIS DAY: Musician Doug Clifford; actor/musician Barbra Streisand; novelist Anthony Trollope

April 25 · **Taurus** · You seek life's deepest mysteries, and this gives you a tolerance that few others possess. At your core is a great spirituality, which gives you amazing strength of character. When disappointment comes your way, you don't lose your composure; instead, you see the challenges as a valuable learning experience.

AVOID: Tension; telling a hurtful truth; worrying about death

ALSO BORN ON THIS DAY: Musician Ella Fitzgerald; basketball star Meadowlark Lemon; journalist Edward R. Murrow

The Bull

April 26 · **Taurus** · There is a serious side to you that isn't always noticeable beneath your amiable exterior. You have fine judgment and possess an instinct for making just the right decision at the opportune time. You take your relationships very seriously, and your ability to inspire sincere affection helps to explain why your friends are so devoted to you. You believe in old-fashioned values. To you, success is always the result of hard work. You have a healthy respect for talent and ability, and you don't think that anything meaningful can be accomplished without sacrifice.

Avoid: Self-interest; emotional detachment; snobbishness

Also born on this day: Artist/naturalist John James Audubon; actor/comedian Carol Burnett; architect I. M. Pei

April 27 · **Taurus** · You are a study in extremes. Your emotions run hot and cold, and you have a reputation for being temperamental when crossed. Though you are intelligent, you are primarily a doer, not a thinker. Instinct plays a big part in guiding your decision-making, and you are famous for saying what you think. You are people-oriented and never seem to run out of enthusiasm. You are a natural cheerleader for worthy causes. Your personality is forceful, sometimes overwhelming, yet your heart is always in the right place. You believe fervently in your dreams and your ability to realize them.

Avoid: Boastfulness; being argumentative; making enemies

Also born on this day: U.S. President Ulysses S. Grant; radio personality Casey Kasem; civil rights activist Coretta Scott King

The Bull

April 28 · **Taurus** · You have an amazing capacity for living
life to the fullest and never fail to recognize an opportunity that
comes your way. People born on this day are firm believers in the
"glass is half full" philosophy. There is no cynicism in your nature,
and you can find logic and reason in even the most difficult and
trying circumstances. You derive a great deal of happiness from
your friends' joys and successes. You tend to identify strongly with
your career, especially if there are other areas of your life that are not
yielding all the promise you expected.

AVOID: Self-pity; laziness; disenchantment

ALSO BORN ON THIS DAY: Actor/entertainer Ann-Margret;
novelist Harper Lee; U.S. President James Monroe

April 29 · **Taurus** · You are concerned with how you are
perceived by others. This isn't the result of an unhealthy ego; rather,
you simply have a high level of sensitivity, and literally "feel" the
approval or disapproval of those around you. Part of the problem is
your inability to appreciate your own best character traits: Learning
to believe wholeheartedly in your own talents can be a tall order
for you. You don't believe in superficial attachments. You are very
loyal to your friends and are willing to go to extremes to offer help
and support. You may be more ambitious than you are comfortable
acknowledging.

AVOID: Irrationality; loose talk; childish behavior

ALSO BORN ON THIS DAY: Musician Duke Ellington; publisher
William Randolph Hearst; comedian Jerry Seinfeld

The Bull

April 30 · **Taurus** · You enjoy living on a big—even massive—scale, with hopes and dreams to match. You are ambitious and are continually working toward success, both personally and professionally. You tend to enjoy playing for high stakes in all aspects of life.

AVOID: Wasting resources; losing interest; self-indulgence

ALSO BORN ON THIS DAY: Actor Eve Arden; actor Cloris Leachman; musician Willie Nelson

May 1 · **Taurus** · You have an indomitable will and endless ambition. Your ambition has little ego attached to it, however, and is primarily a vehicle for the expression of personality. Your energy inspires everyone around you. You are a natural leader.

AVOID: Lack of communication; competition; loneliness

ALSO BORN ON THIS DAY: Actor Glenn Ford; novelist Joseph Heller; musician Tim McGraw

May 2 · **Taurus** · You are fully aware of your unique gifts and want to share them with the world. Creativity—both artistic and intellectual—is your personal hallmark. Although you may seem cautious, you are an adventurous soul. You are brave about the choices you make in life.

AVOID: Being docile; deception; incompatibility

ALSO BORN ON THIS DAY: Musician Jon Bon Jovi; satirist Jerome K. Jerome; renowned pediatrician Dr. Benjamin Spock

The Bull

May 3 · **Taurus** ·

Power, and the means by which it is used and exchanged, are central factors in defining your life. You continually find yourself drawn to the very seat of power, though you may not desire to occupy it yourself. You want very much to help others through your own experiences, but first you must come to grips with some of the truths in your life. You are determined to make good use of all the opportunities that come your way and tend to be drawn toward work that improves the lives of everyone in your community. Not particularly intuitive, you depend upon logic to point the way.

AVOID: Material gratification; emotional isolation; chaos

ALSO BORN ON THIS DAY: Musicians James Brown, Bing Crosby, and Pete Seeger

May 4 · **Taurus** ·

Where most people have a tendency to complicate events, you want to enjoy life in a simple and unadorned fashion. Although it may take many years for you to throw off the burdens that keep you from exploring life on your own terms, you will eventually come to this point of view. You have a charismatic personality that sets you apart. You are a philosophical type who asks "Why not?" when contemplating a life change. You tend to work harder in aid of others than for yourself. Just as you don't flaunt your possessions, neither do you make a great display of your charitable works. You often choose to do good work in silence.

AVOID: Anxiety; insecurity; drawing conclusions

ALSO BORN ON THIS DAY: Sportscaster Erin Andrews; actor Will Arnett; actor Audrey Hepburn

The Bull

May 5 · **Taurus** · Individuals born on this day have a definite
agenda in mind. You are verbal, imaginative, and not at all shy about
expressing your opinions. You are also a good listener, and despite
your "chatty" reputation, you can keep a secret better than most
people. You identify more with your intellect than with any other
aspect of your nature. You never stop learning, never want to close
the book on achieving the very best you can. You are adventurous,
and you are looking to establish a "personal best" that accords with
your own standards—not those of anyone else.

AVOID: Living in a dream world; glib remarks; apathy

ALSO BORN ON THIS DAY: Journalist Nellie Bly; political
philosopher Karl Marx; TV journalist Brian Williams

May 6 · **Taurus** · Where life goals are concerned, many people
born on this date are late starters. You coast through the first half of
your life on charm and show your grit only after you've weathered
a few disappointments. What you really want most is to be taken
seriously. You must find a way to transcend your physical appeal.
You have unique creative talents and special ways of displaying your
artistic vision. May 6 individuals are usually trailblazers rather than
traditionalists. There is often a fairy-tale element in the romantic
lives of May 6 people. No matter what happens, they never lose the
ability to believe in love's wondrous magic.

AVOID: Pretense; empty promises; casual sex

ALSO BORN ON THIS DAY: Psychoanalysis founder Sigmund
Freud; actor Rudolph Valentino; baseball star Willie Mays

The Bull

May 7 · **Taurus** · You know how to love, how to serve, and how to wait. You are highly principled, and your concern for others typically outweighs concern for yourself. Your ability to put your own quiet strength behind the people you love is remarkable. You tend to keep your hopes and dreams to yourself.

AVOID: Idle talk; envying others; ill-mannered behavior

ALSO BORN ON THIS DAY: Poet Robert Browning; composer Pyotr Ilich Tchaikovsky; football star Johnny Unitas

May 8 · **Taurus** · You are practical and intelligent in a commonsense way. While not glamorous, you have the opportunity to make a name for yourself by your capableness. You can recognize the funny side of any situation, and you have a reputation for saying what you think, whether it's critical or complimentary.

AVOID: Pressure; nervousness; loneliness

ALSO BORN ON THIS DAY: Naturalist David Attenborough; novelist Peter Benchley; U.S. President Harry S. Truman

May 9 · **Taurus** · You possess a bold spirit that propels you toward challenges that most individuals would never face. Despite the forcefulness of your personality, you are not pushy. You are very enthusiastic, and you have the ability to laugh at yourself.

AVOID: Preoccupation with death; boredom; pretentiousness

ALSO BORN ON THIS DAY: Author J. M. Barrie; filmmaker/writer James L. Brooks; musician Billy Joel

The Bull

May 10 · **Taurus** · You have a special view of the world. You are a cautious optimist and believe that if you try hard enough, you can make a positive impact upon your world. Though you aren't naturally a solitary person, you require a lot of privacy. You live out your dreams and goals on an everyday basis, relying on your subconscious for guidance. Because you do not enjoy taking instruction from others, you tend to work alone or behind the scenes. You have very high expectations about your ability to turn failure into success, and you may sometimes subconsciously hinder your own efforts in order to test your ability to "come back."

AVOID: Risky behavior; naïveté; shame

ALSO BORN ON THIS DAY: Dancer/actor Fred Astaire; musician Bono; film-score composer Max Steiner

May 11 · **Taurus** · Few people have the overwhelming creative potential that you possess. Whether or not you turn your talents toward artistic expression, you will be known for your ability to turn the ordinary into the special. You are brilliant, talented—and somewhat volatile. Despite a reputation for being short-tempered, even critical, you command the loyalty and devotion of everyone who knows you. There is no limit to how big you can dream. You believe in your talent, and you have far more grit than is generally supposed.

AVOID: Negative influences; grudges; favoritism

ALSO BORN ON THIS DAY: Songwriter Irving Berlin; pilot Harriet Quimby; actor Natasha Richardson

The Bull

May 12 · Taurus · You are not so much a leader as you are

a guide, eager to show others the world through your eyes. You appreciate the serious aspects of life, even though you seem to be caught up in the pure pleasure of living it. You have boundless energy and give equal amounts to both work and play. You believe in setting reachable goals. Your enjoyment and enthusiasm show in everything you do. Although you don't need to be the center of attention, you generally are. Many of your associates try to emulate your charm and good-natured appeal.

AVOID: Repetition; sarcasm; becoming notorious

ALSO BORN ON THIS DAY: Composer Burt Bacharach; actor Katharine Hepburn; poet Edward Lear

May 13 · Taurus · You are a rare individual with unique and

special talents. You have great imaginative potential, which you may need to shape through learning and experience. You have a naturally giving nature and the ability to put your trust in someone close to you. You are quick to reveal your thoughts and feelings, and you enjoy talking about shared goals. Because you tend to judge with your heart instead of your head, you should take romantic relationships slowly. To be better able to accomplish your goals, keep a specific direction in mind. There is a dark side to you, yet you are rarely moved to show this aspect of yourself to anyone.

AVOID: Senseless arguments; overspending; tension

ALSO BORN ON THIS DAY: Comedian/satirist Stephen Colbert; novelist Daphne Du Maurier; musician Stevie Wonder

The Bull

May 14 · **Taurus** · You are torn between the intellectual life
you are drawn to and the active life you also want to pursue. You
have extraordinary artistic vision and can do great things if left to
your own devices. You love to bounce your ideas off others, enjoying
the give-and-take of differing opinions.

AVOID: Rage; confusion; lack of imagination

ALSO BORN ON THIS DAY: Musician Bobby Darin; filmmaker
George Lucas; Facebook.com founder Mark Zuckerberg

May 15 · **Taurus** · You draw inspiration from your
surroundings. You have a great need to distill your experience and
share it with others through personal expression. You like to feel
thoroughly connected to the world family.

AVOID: Bitterness; emotional stability; lies

ALSO BORN ON THIS DAY: Secretary of State Madeleine Albright;
novelist L. Frank Baum; baseball star George Brett

May 16 · **Taurus** · You are among the most buoyant and
fascinating personalities within the entire spectrum of astrology. You
have your own view of life and your own style. You are an innovator
and value your freedom of choice above everything else. You see no
point in maintaining tradition just for its own sake.

AVOID: Picking fights with friends; attitude problems; shallowness

ALSO BORN ON THIS DAY: Actor Henry Fonda; gymnast Olga
Korbut; designer Christian Lacroix

The Bull

May 17 · **Taurus** · You enjoy the pursuit of excellence. You are a self-starter, and you know what you want and how to get it. You will not allow yourself to be diverted from achieving your goals. You are intelligent, though not showy about what you know; for this reason, you may not be perceived as especially brilliant by others. That's fine with you, since you are considerably less concerned with how your actions are perceived by others than with whether you yourself are content. Because you have considerable leadership potential, you are likely to surround yourself with more "followers" than equals.

AVOID: Inconsistency; guilt; cruelty

ALSO BORN ON THIS DAY: Watergate prosecutor Archibald Cox; actor Dennis Hopper; boxer Sugar Ray Leonard

May 18 · **Taurus** · You love freedom and independence. You are temperamental, lovable, and exasperating; you make it impossible for others to be indifferent toward you. You possess extraordinary creative energy and are never without an important cause to champion. You enjoy taking risks, but only when you believe the risk "matters." You are deceptively ambitious—a fact that may go unnoticed by everyone except those who know you best. You are extremely emotional and no stranger to heartache. You are wise and understand that heartache often brings a measure of wisdom.

AVOID: Rationalization; anxiety; feeling guilty

ALSO BORN ON THIS DAY: Filmmaker Frank Capra; actor/comedian Tina Fey; Pope John Paul II

The Bull

May 19 · Taurus · You came into this world wanting to change it. You are extremely motivated, eager to put your personal stamp upon your environment. You have supreme confidence in your abilities and never shrink when it comes to doing what is expected of you. You are a loner, but not in the traditional sense. You enjoy being with people, yet you trust only your own counsel and rarely take the advice of others. Resourceful? You're at the head of the line. That old adage "there are no small parts, only small actors" could have been written to describe you.

AVOID: Nightmares; taking foolish chances; losing faith

ALSO BORN ON THIS DAY: Screenwriter/filmmaker Nora Ephron; explorer Ferdinand Magellan; activist Malcolm X

May 20 · Taurus · You have a streak of eccentricity in your otherwise conventional personality. You seem to draw friends from all walks of life. You love to listen to anyone's story and are famous for giving remarkably apt advice. You have a need to display your talents on a very large scale, yet this may be in conflict with your basic need for emotional privacy. You are ambitious, yet you may lack the emotional stamina needed to be successful in your chosen field. You may have an unrealistic attitude about what it takes to make your dreams come true.

AVOID: Negative attitude; running away from problems; lack of respect for reasonable authority

ALSO BORN ON THIS DAY: Actor/musician Cher; philosopher John Stuart Mill; actor Jimmy Stewart

The Twins

May 21 · **Gemini** · You have a great will to succeed, and you bend all your efforts toward that aim. Although you may not be especially good at articulating your goals, you have a very clear idea of what you want out of life. Security is usually very high on the list, and you will work hard to ensure it. You see things on a grand—even epic—scale and live your life in a similar fashion. Because of your dedication and sense of purpose, you may be perceived as ruthless at times. However, you are extremely generous and always willing to help out.

AVOID: Backtracking; irascibility; inflated speech

ALSO BORN ON THIS DAY: Actor Raymond Burr; artist Henri Rousseau; actor Mr. T

May 22 · **Gemini** · You are unique in the extreme. You have great charisma and the ability to draw attention to yourself. You possess something of a dual nature: You may be lofty and intellectual one day, earthy and intense on another. You are generally seen as a leader, though you may not see yourself in this role. You are proud to see your hard work rewarded. You don't believe in getting something for nothing and would not wish to have idle dreams come true. But when you work very hard toward a goal—especially if it requires the discipline of many years—you are ecstatic when you succeed.

AVOID: Being quarrelsome; self-interest; obsession

ALSO BORN ON THIS DAY: Artist Mary Cassat; writer Sir Arthur Conan Doyle; actor Sir Laurence Olivier

The Twins

May 23 · **Gemini** · People born on May 23 are known for their sense of humor and sense of style. You are fun-loving and free-thinking, and you enjoy life on your terms. Even more than most Geminians, you embody a youthful attitude. You are highly idealistic and spend a great deal of time daydreaming.

AVOID: Artifice; risky behavior; dwelling on bad memories

ALSO BORN ON THIS DAY: Writer Mitch Albom; silent film actor Douglas Fairbanks Sr.; musician Jewel

Ⅱ

May 24 · **Gemini** · Despite the placid face you turn to the world, you have rock-hard opinions. You are well suited to handling the stresses of life, even though you may appear to be fragile. You usually get your way, though you do it with subtlety and diplomacy.

AVOID: Emotional temptation; ego trips; giving in to writer's block

ALSO BORN ON THIS DAY: Musician Rosanne Cash; musician Bob Dylan; Queen Victoria of Great Britain

Ⅱ

May 25 · **Gemini** · You enjoy being in life's fast lane. You have enormous ambition and put career ahead of relationships. You are creative in a quirky way, preferring to put your unique spin on projects.

AVOID: Jealousy; carelessness with money; putting off necessary chores

ALSO BORN ON THIS DAY: Novelist Robert Ludlum; actor Sir Ian McKellen; opera singer Beverly Sills

Ⅱ

The Twins

May 26 · **Gemini** · Your natural character is hard for others to divine. Outwardly you appear serious—even stoic. Yet underneath it all, you are warm-hearted, kind, and even funny when the mood strikes you. You are very aware of your own dignity. Even the way you carry yourself proclaims a sense of decorum. Friendship is one of the most important factors in your life, and you have a knack for making very close friendships that can last a lifetime. You are extremely loyal and would do anything for a friend. You understand that very few goals can be achieved overnight. You have the foresight and patience to achieve your dreams one step at a time.

AVOID: Being overly practical; estrangement from friends; self-pity

ALSO BORN ON THIS DAY: Actor Helena Bonham Carter; musician Miles Davis; astronaut Sally Ride

May 27 · **Gemini** · You are a master at reinventing yourself. This is your way of remaining interesting to yourself and others. You never quite let anyone see your true self—not even those individuals closest to you. You love the spotlight and especially enjoy situations where you can meet new and interesting people. You like eccentric people who share your love of good food and smart conversation. You will usually find a way to shine, since anything less is unbearable to your ego. You are a natural flirt, and you generally prefer "the chase" to any other aspect of love.

AVOID: Intimidation; snobbishness; misinformation

ALSO BORN ON THIS DAY: Writer Dashiell Hammett; actor Vincent Price; golf champion Sam Snead

The Twins

May 28 · Gemini · You possess an adventurous pioneer spirit.

You don't wait for life to happen to you—you go out and wrestle with it. You never lose interest in life, and you are confident in your ability to conquer it. Enthusiastic and fun-loving, you are a great friend. You count your successes according to the number of lives you touch and people you inspire—and how much fun everybody has along the way. You believe in performing selfless acts of charity that improve the lives of others. This, combined with unstinting good humor, is your trademark.

AVOID: Bad dreams; revenge; nervousness

ALSO BORN ON THIS DAY: Novelist Ian Fleming; politician Rudy Giuliani; Olympian Jim Thorpe

Ⅱ

May 29 · Gemini · You possess charm, intelligence, wit, and

a star quality that is virtually unrivaled. Your ability to sway the opinions of others is nothing short of miraculous. If you lack for anything, it is an introspective side. You prefer not to analyze your feelings except on rare occasions. You gravitate to risk and can even be foolhardy at times. You are extremely goal-oriented and will work very hard to make a goal become a reality. If you get bored along the way, however, you will toss all your hard work to the wind without a second thought.

AVOID: Not taking yourself seriously enough; aloofness; overlooking areas that need your attention

ALSO BORN ON THIS DAY: Actor Annette Bening; musician Noel Gallagher; American patriot Patrick Henry

Ⅱ

The Twins

May 30 · **Gemini** · You see the entire world as your canvas. You have considerable mettle and can overcome adversity with ease. You bring a great sense of joy and comfort to all your relationships. Your will to succeed is strong but never ruthless. You have a knack for organization and are scrupulously honest.

AVOID: Indifference; sleeplessness; poor choices

ALSO BORN ON THIS DAY: Musician Benny Goodman; filmmaker Howard Hawks; musician Wynonna Judd

Ⅱ

May 31 · **Gemini** · You like to push the proverbial envelope, always looking for ways to get close to dangerous circumstances without actually getting hurt. You like to give others the impression that you have a "bad" streak, but—generally speaking—you're not as unconventional as you may appear.

AVOID: The need for validation; no-win situations; giving up

ALSO BORN ON THIS DAY: Actor/filmmaker Clint Eastwood; Prince Rainier of Monaco; poet Walt Whitman

Ⅱ

June 1 · **Gemini** · You have a great need to bask in the sun of approval. You value your talents and abilities, yet you constantly look to your peers for validation and advice. Feeling that you have the power to please others is as seductive to you as your own success.

AVOID: Being overly dependent; empty promises; scheming

ALSO BORN ON THIS DAY: Musician Pat Boone; actor Morgan Freeman; actor Marilyn Monroe

Ⅱ

The Twins

June 2 · Gemini · You live more through your emotions than your intellect. This may not be readily apparent, since you are a bright achiever with a quiet personality that discourages you from "opening up"; you reserve your real self for those closest to you. You have a more serious disposition than many Geminians. You give the impression of being emotionally fragile, but you are actually very strong-willed and independent. You are not interested in superficial relationships of any sort; to the contrary, you seek out friends who can share your need for emotional intimacy.

AVOID: Doubts; constant criticism (of self and others); gloating

ALSO BORN ON THIS DAY: Composer Sir Edward Elgar; novelist Thomas Hardy; activist Cornel West

♊

June 3 · Gemini · People born on June 3 are extremely intelligent, though their brilliance is likely to be analytical rather than creative in nature. You are much more at home analyzing abstract issues rather than handling life's more commonplace problems. You have considerable nervous energy, which can manifest itself as ill temper. Although you can be argumentative at times, you are much more likely to keep your feelings to yourself. There is an element of egotism in your persona, yet it does not detract from your likability. Friends admire your intellect. It's important to you that you achieve a level of independence in your personal and professional life.

AVOID: Selfishness; emotional power plays; needless fear

ALSO BORN ON THIS DAY: TV journalist Anderson Cooper; actor Tony Curtis; musician Curtis Mayfield

♊

The Twins

June 4 • **Gemini** • You think of life as one big series of exciting surprises, and you are not afraid to take chances or reinvent yourself from time to time. You combine daring with practicality, discipline with artistry. This all comes naturally to you because of your incredible ability to see things from multiple perspectives. You have a sparkling personality and are very much aware of the effect you have on others. You love spontaneity and would rather be caught off guard by circumstances than plan for them. One of your greatest traits is your humanitarianism—you feel it is your duty to give your resources and talents to help those who are less fortunate.

AVOID: Giving in to disillusionment; scheming; codependency

ALSO BORN ON THIS DAY: Opera singer Cecilia Bartoli; George III of Great Britain; actor Angelina Jolie

June 5 • **Gemini** • You believe in the natural goodness of the world around you, and you have a remarkable ability to see things in a positive light. You are excited about life and want to experience everything it has to offer. You are more than merely optimistic— you are an altruist who draws your greatest inspiration from the magic of everyday life that others may not perceive. You like being surrounded by good companions and rarely prefer your own company to that of friends. Your goals are optimistic in nature— sometimes impossibly so. But this does not deter you. If a dream does not come true, you simply turn your attention to the next goal.

AVOID: Wasting time; judging others; letting tasks overwhelm you

ALSO BORN ON THIS DAY: Musician Kenny G; economist John Maynard Keynes; journalist Bill Moyers

The Twins

June 6 · **Gemini** · You are a remarkable individual for whom the world is one gigantic wonder to be explored. You have unbounded curiosity and never tire of learning new things. You understand what many people do not: that the journey is more important than the destination.

AVOID: Tension; negativity; hopelessness

ALSO BORN ON THIS DAY: Comedian Sandra Bernhard; tennis star Björn Borg; actor Paul Giamatti

June 7 · **Gemini** · You yearn to make your presence felt in the world, and you can get far in life just on your charm. You are curious and vibrant, with an ability to keep your level of enthusiasm high no matter what obstacles you encounter.

AVOID: Greed; envy; dishonor

ALSO BORN ON THIS DAY: Basketball star Allen Iverson; musician Prince; actor Jessica Tandy

June 8 · **Gemini** · You are a survivor, with considerably more emotional stamina than the typical Gemini. No matter how many times you suffer setbacks or disappointments, you come back and start again. You are a hard worker and put your whole heart and soul into everything you do. Your level of commitment is amazing.

AVOID: Pretense; laziness; giving in to discouragement

ALSO BORN ON THIS DAY: American politician Gabrielle Giffords; actor Julianna Margulies; architect Frank Lloyd Wright

The Twins

June 9 · Gemini · You are motivated to succeed in every

aspect of life. You are excitable and imaginative, with a great sense of humor. Like most Geminians, you are talkative and enjoy a rousing debate about a variety of subjects. You can have a good time in just about any situation; in fact, you are often the proverbial life of the party. You also have a serious side, but you usually keep it hidden. You use bold intelligence to put your plans into action from a very early age, and you have the daring to undertake risks that would intimidate other people.

AVOID: Self-pity; bossiness; manipulative people

ALSO BORN ON THIS DAY: Actors Johnny Depp, Michael J. Fox, and Natalie Portman

♊

June 10 · Gemini · You have a highly emotional nature.

You may seem to be on an endless roller coaster of highs and lows, which can both amaze and alarm those close to you. Although you seem very secure with your self-image, you are acutely aware of the expectations of others and may often go to great lengths to live up to them. Being at ease with who you are is a trait that you will need to cultivate. You have a great many goals and plans, yet you may not always feel confident you have what it takes to realize them. You find it difficult to be truly happy unless you feel fulfilled on an emotional level as well as a spiritual one.

AVOID: Excesses; unstable love affairs; depression

ALSO BORN ON THIS DAY: Author Saul Bellow; Olympian Tara Lipinski; author Maurice Sendak

♊

The Twins

June 11 · **Gemini** · Although you are not particularly goal-oriented, you have a strong personal vision about what you want your life to be. You know what you want out of life, and you have the ability to move beyond the commonplace. Even though you need a great deal of personal validation from others, you generally possess an ego strong enough to support your grandiose ambitions. You have leadership qualities that are second to none. Properly focused, you have the potential to make a real difference in the world. You have a great deal of faith in your own abilities and will work very hard to make your dreams come true.

Avoid: Going to extremes; dogmatic behavior; hypocrisy

Also born on this day: Football coach Vince Lombardi; health expert Dr. Mehmet Öz; actor/filmmaker Gene Wilder

Ⅱ

June 12 · **Gemini** · You are a big thinker with the enthusiasm to go for broke. You see the big picture and have a great love of life. You are an incredible optimist and believe that everything that happens is for the best. When you must face a setback, you are never discouraged. You are a great self-starter and always seem to have a plan in mind. June 12 individuals usually hold career positions that allow them to act as leaders. You have a genuine love of people and value diversity in your circle of pals. You are very serious about romantic commitments and seldom break them.

Avoid: Seeking out confrontation; poor choices; materialism

Also born on this day: U.S. President George H. W. Bush; historian/writer Anne Frank; baseball star Hideki Matsui

Ⅱ

The Twins

June 13 · **Gemini** · You are drawn to adventure and prefer living on the edge. You have no patience with people who make only "safe" choices. You will always set your sights on what you want and go after it, no matter what it takes. You have a kinetic kind of charm that easily draws others to you.

AVOID: Feeling insecure; rage; guilt feelings

ALSO BORN ON THIS DAY: Actor Tim Allen; actor Malcolm McDowell; poet William Butler Yeats

June 14 · **Gemini** · You are in a class by yourself. You combine a winning personality with a penetrating intelligence that is truly disarming. You are a social gadfly, and you are never shy about expressing your opinions.

AVOID: Arrogance; self-doubt; being argumentative

ALSO BORN ON THIS DAY: Musician Boy George; photographer Margaret Bourke-White; tennis star Steffi Graf

June 15 · **Gemini** · You know how to get your way with charm. Even though you're tough, you are never rude or abrasive. You possess the proverbial iron fist in a velvet glove. Even when you choose to play hardball with an opponent or rival, the individual in question may never realize they've been in a fight.

AVOID: Playing favorites; indecisiveness; incompatibility

ALSO BORN ON THIS DAY: Psychologist Erik Erikson; actor Neil Patrick Harris; musician Waylon Jennings

The Twins

June 16 · Gemini ·
Enthusiasm and a genuine curiosity about life mark your personality. You are a true adventurer—to you, every day is a potential voyage of discovery. You have strong opinions yet are always open to new experiences. You have great people skills and make an exceptionally fine host at social gatherings. You are perceptive, bright, and as interested in those around you as in your own concerns. Communication is the keynote to any career sought by June 16 people. You enjoy spontaneity and are often reluctant to plot a course of action. You believe very much in the benevolence of time and enjoy taking each day as it comes.

AVOID: Manipulative people; extreme thrills; bickering

ALSO BORN ON THIS DAY: Apache leader Geronimo; comedian Stan Laurel; writer Joyce Carol Oates

June 17 · Gemini ·
Unlike most Geminians, people born on this day are uncharacteristically serious. You are very concerned with being a success in life, yet a spirit of rebellion lurks behind your seemingly conservative and traditional surface. You have a vision all your own, but you aren't always sure just how to achieve it. You are concerned about stepping out of character and letting others see your vulnerabilities, and you have difficulty confiding your feelings to others. This, however, is exactly what you need to do to come to grips with your true nature.

AVOID: Excessive daydreaming; irresponsibility; ingratitude

ALSO BORN ON THIS DAY: Artist M. C. Escher; musician Barry Manilow; tennis star Venus Williams

The Twins

June 18 · **Gemini** · You are a sensible individual with high ambitions and clear ideas about what you want to achieve. It is very important for you to make a success of your life. You keep busy and never seem to have a moment of leisure at your disposal.

AVOID: Ruthlessness; stubbornness; ill humor

ALSO BORN ON THIS DAY: Film critic Roger Ebert; musician Sir Paul McCartney; musician Blake Shelton

June 19 · **Gemini** · You love being first in everything. You adore being in the spotlight and will fight to stay there. You are goal-oriented rather than egotistical; you know your own worth and are eager to prove it. You have personality to spare and are not shy about displaying it.

AVOID: Wallowing in sadness; selfishness; being easily discouraged

ALSO BORN ON THIS DAY: Baseball star Lou Gehrig; film critic Pauline Kael; mathematician Blaise Pascal

June 20 · **Gemini** · You have a unique and interesting character. An attitude of emotional instability makes you very attractive to others; they may feel a need to "take care" of you, although you are actually much more centered than you appear. You want true happiness and will unfailingly seek it out.

AVOID: Anger issues; unpredictable behavior; mood swings

ALSO BORN ON THIS DAY: Actor John Goodman; author Lillian Hellman; actor Nicole Kidman

The Crab

June 21 · **Cancer** · People born on this day feel the need to do great good in the world. You are happy individuals with a genuine love for others. Fairness is a passion with you, and you have a personal need to live according to a set of ethical standards. You are talented and far-thinking, and your intelligence is combined with a great sense of caring. You do not shrink from becoming involved in situations that put your reputation on the line. You have a wide and varied set of friends who allow you to see life from ever-changing perspectives. You live large and dream large, always believing in your ability to make your goals come true.

AVOID: Pettiness; revenge; feelings of alienation

ALSO BORN ON THIS DAY: Philosopher Jean-Paul Sartre; filmmaker Tony Scott; Prince William, Duke of Cambridge

June 22 · **Cancer** · You may be perceived as being sociable, but you are actually very shy and seek your own company as much as possible. You are extremely sensitive to the emotional climate around you and can be both positively and negatively affected by it. You have a secret side, which you show only to those closest to you. Not given to displays of ego, you prefer to remain in the background, where you perform your daily responsibilities expertly and in your own quiet way. One of your premier aims is to do as much good for others as possible.

AVOID: Deception; lecturing subordinates; feelings of superiority

ALSO BORN ON THIS DAY: Politician Diane Feinstein; actor Meryl Streep; filmmaker Billy Wilder

The Crab

June 23 · Cancer ·

The people born on this date know how to have a good time. You are likely to be less serious and sensitive than most men and women born under the sign of Cancer. You are generous, loyal, and have a heartfelt concern for others. You are an intelligent, commonsense type with an unexpected streak of eccentricity. You appreciate a funny story when you hear one and have a reputation for playing practical jokes on your closest friends and family members. You strive to achieve all that life can give you, and you continue to be thrilled and challenged by your future.

AVOID: Insensitivity; lack of humility; bossiness

ALSO BORN ON THIS DAY: Researcher Alfred Kinsey; actor Frances McDormand; Olympian Wilma Rudolph

June 24 · Cancer ·

You have great personal charm, which may give others the impression that you are less driven than you actually are. In fact, you are extremely career-oriented, and you've been known to sacrifice personal happiness to achieve your aims. You often take circuitous paths toward your goals, becoming involved in or distracted by other aims in the process. Yet once you see the possibility of a dream coming true, nothing can keep you from attaining it. You have a great need to break with tradition and the past. Creative and artistic, you feel you have something to prove to yourself and others, and you won't abandon that goal at any cost.

AVOID: Costly mistakes in love; economic stress; jealousy

ALSO BORN ON THIS DAY: Musician Jeff Beck; writer Ambrose Bierce; boxer Jack Dempsey

The Crab

June 25 · **Cancer** · You are unusually sensitive and apt to find yourself at odds with your true nature and the bold person you hope to be. You emit a dreamy and inexact persona, leading others to believe (often incorrectly) that you are not very focused.

AVOID: Risky choices; anger; petty limitations

ALSO BORN ON THIS DAY: Musician George Michael; novelist George Orwell; U.S. Supreme Court Justice Sonia Sotomayor

June 26 · **Cancer** · You are blessed with a brilliant and creative mind and a powerful personality that attracts others. You have extraordinary potential. Under your calm and quiet surface is a wicked sense of humor that can cut your scholarly reputation—and the pretensions of others—to ribbons.

AVOID: Insincerity; dwelling on heartache; wallowing in self-pity

ALSO BORN ON THIS DAY: Author Pearl S. Buck; baseball star Derek Jeter; athlete Babe Didrikson Zaharias

June 27 · **Cancer** · Although you possess a great sense of your own importance, you are not egotistical. You have a strong, imperious personality, yet you wear it with ease and grace and exude a dynamic charm. You are upbeat, friendly, and devoted to creating meaningful friendships.

AVOID: Envy; being disrespectful; self-pity

ALSO BORN ON THIS DAY: Writer Helen Keller; actor Tobey Maguire; U.S. presidential candidate/businessman Ross Perot

The Crab

June 28 · **Cancer** · You have a marvelous sense of fun. This isn't just a sense of humor, but a way in which you choose to live life. If you can't have fun with a situation, you don't want to be involved in it. You are determined to wring every bit of humor out of even the most unlikely events. You are democratic in your attitude and can laugh at yourself. Although you are witty and hilarious, you are far from lighthearted at your core. You have very few close confidantes, and you seldom open yourself up emotionally, even to those closest to you. You need to be careful about erecting unnecessary emotional barriers.

AVOID: Hasty actions; hurting others; deceit

ALSO BORN ON THIS DAY: Actor Kathy Bates; comedian/filmmaker Mel Brooks; King Henry VIII of England

June 29 · **Cancer** · There is something almost preternaturally sensitive about the men and women born on this date. You are ruled more by emotion than reason, and you refuse to give up your idealism even in the face of hard facts and realism. Yet you are far more determined than your nature would make you seem. You have a great reservoir of faith and strength, which allows you to move forward despite trouble. You care about helping others. You are unselfish and always involved in some activity that brings hope or inspiration to others.

AVOID: Guilt; self-doubt; needy people

ALSO BORN ON THIS DAY: Actor Maria Conchita Alonso; musician Nelson Eddy; film producer Robert Evans

The Crab

June 30 · Cancer · You have an exceptionally well-balanced nature. You are materialistic, yet in a good sense because you wish to help others. At the same time, you'll never neglect the welfare of those closest to you. You are sensible, yet fun-loving. You strive for success yet never lose sight of your personal commitments. You are strongly motivated to serve the greater good. You believe you can achieve whatever you want in life. This positive attitude is a self-fulfilling prophecy, because your dreams often come true. In the rare instances when one of your dreams is not realized, you have the resilience to adopt a philosophical attitude.

AVOID: Being judgmental; greed; sense of superiority

ALSO BORN ON THIS DAY: Musician Lena Horne; Olympian Michael Phelps; boxer Mike Tyson

July 1 · Cancer · Because you are naturally shy, you often prefer to work behind the scenes, letting others take the bows you are too timid to take. You are a wonderful humanitarian, and the gratification you receive by helping others is more valuable to you than any material consideration. You strive for perfection and have an unfortunate knack for being your own worst enemy. Even though you are good-hearted and generous, you seem to draw complications and controversy into your midst. You seem to have great emotional fragility, but your spirit is actually very strong.

AVOID: Self-criticism; self-consciousness; destructive habits

ALSO BORN ON THIS DAY: Princess Diana; Olympian Carl Lewis; novelist George Sand

The Crab

July 2 · **Cancer** · You know how to use humor as both a tool and a weapon. You will always find a way to use your abilities to shine. You believe in yourself and try to do the very best you can to live up to your potential.

AVOID: Stinginess; lack of imagination; stubbornness

ALSO BORN ON THIS DAY: Actor/TV producer Larry David; novelist Hermann Hesse; U.S. Supreme Court Justice Thurgood Marshall

July 3 · **Cancer** · Though you may seem conventional on the surface, you have a deeply mystical nature. You live life according to your own personal vision. At once eccentric and blessed with exceptionally good taste, you enjoy living the good life but never lose sight of your spiritual concerns.

AVOID: Intolerance; immaturity; lack of focus

ALSO BORN ON THIS DAY: Actor Tom Cruise; novelist Franz Kafka; playwright Tom Stoppard

July 4 · **Cancer** · You are strong-willed, dedicated to having your way, but you are also fair enough to admit when you are wrong. You have a humanitarian streak and will do many good deeds in your life, yet you prefer doing that work secretly.

AVOID: Materialism; ingratitude; weak character

ALSO BORN ON THIS DAY: U.S. President Calvin Coolidge; novelist Nathaniel Hawthorne; playwright Neil Simon

The Crab

July 5 · Cancer · You need a large stage on which to live your life. You have a profound need to live in the "now," and yet you desire to transcend time through your own actions and plans. Intelligent, shrewd, and canny, you put your own stamp on events. You can talk yourself into almost any situation and impress others with your insightful thinking. Despite a strong cynical streak, your innate openness to others makes it easy for people to like you. You are ambitious but may not possess the self-discipline to see goals through to fruition.

AVOID: Emotional depletion; self-pity; bluntness

ALSO BORN ON THIS DAY: Circus owner P. T. Barnum; actor Edie Falco; politician Henry Cabot Lodge

July 6 · Cancer · You have a great love of comfort and beauty. You draw immense pleasure from a well-decorated and harmoniously maintained environment. While status often plays a big role in your need to be surrounded by luxury, you are basically a down-to-earth person and derive a great deal of pleasure from being able to help those with fewer resources. You can be excessively demanding in your personal relationships. You don't like to share your friends with outsiders and may seem bossy when it comes to giving advice or suggestions. You seek happiness and accomplishment through relationships with the people you love.

AVOID: Pretense; snobbishness; always needing to win

ALSO BORN ON THIS DAY: The Dalai Lama of Tibet; rock 'n' roll legend Bill Haley; artist Frida Kahlo

The Crab

July 7 · **Cancer** · People born on July 7 often feel the need to change the world they were born into. You are a visionary filled with artistic dreams, and the idea of being able to share your special talents with others holds great excitement for you. Dedicated to self-improvement in all its forms, you understand that the greatest lessons in life take place on a subconscious level. You have the potential for great spirituality but may spend a great deal of your life confused as to what you actually believe. You are not shy about letting others feel the influence of your own religious faith or spiritual conscience.

AVOID: Anger; guile; playing with people's feelings

ALSO BORN ON THIS DAY: Artist Marc Chagall; Olympian Michelle Kwan; musician Ringo Starr

July 8 · **Cancer** · Your quirky personality gives you a carefree, eccentric aspect, but in truth you are more serious-minded than you appear. You believe in conquering the "impossible dream" and have a powerful need to display your abilities. Your idealistic streak is powerful, but you don't expect things to come to you easily. You understand that there must sometimes be a trade-off between what you want and what you can have. You know the worth of personal goals, and you understand that money and possessions mean little unless loved ones are around to share these things.

AVOID: Prejudice; patronizing remarks; cheating

ALSO BORN ON THIS DAY: Actor Kevin Bacon; actor Anjelica Huston; author Anna Quindlen

The Crab

July 9 · **Cancer** · You are ambitious, positive, and eager to succeed. You are a great role model. You have the ability to be happy with few material possessions, yet because you're willing to think more of others than yourself, you often receive blessings many times over.

Avoid: Negativity; jealousy; controversial issues

Also born on this day: Actor Tom Hanks; artist David Hockney; actor Jimmy Smits

July 10 · **Cancer** · You are far more conventional than you appear. Although willful, you also possess considerable self-discipline. Your natural authoritarian streak is balanced by a need to have the good opinion of others in order to be happy.

Avoid: Manipulation; gossip; bad manners

Also born on this day: Tennis star Arthur Ashe; actor Sofia Vergara; artist James Whistler

July 11 · **Cancer** · Kind and generous, you use your extreme sensitivity to understand others. You may not always appear to be on top of the world because your happy nature is something you often keep within yourself.

Avoid: Excessive solitude; dwelling on unhappy memories; harmful associations

Also born on this day: U.S. President John Quincy Adams; actor Yul Brynner; writer E. B. White

The Crab

July 12 · **Cancer** · You are a partier who manages to retain a set of values and a strong humanitarian streak. An inner emotional pain encourages you to bring happiness to others. In this way, you're able to make yourself happy. You don't simply want to help others—you need to do so. You have a great need to connect with others on a profoundly emotional level. Even though you have a love of material things, you understand the spiritual realm as well. You are energized by people and genuinely care for others, and you make friends wherever you go. People appreciate your tolerant viewpoint and appreciation and respect for the beliefs of others.

AVOID: Cynicism; lack of focus; fair-weather friends

ALSO BORN ON THIS DAY: Actor/comedian Bill Cosby; writer Henry David Thoreau; Olympian Kristi Yamaguchi

July 13 · **Cancer** · You are blessed with a charismatic personality that complements your gentle soul. Modest, you often receive far more attention than you are comfortable with. You have a fear of change, yet you understand that it is only through change that you are able to discover your own true nature. You have high ideals, and you're anxious to fulfill them. If you can influence others positively through your words or actions, you feel as if your fondest wish has come true. When you have a deeply personal goal, you're unlikely to share it with anyone else.

AVOID: Vacillation; foolish choices; allowing others' disapproval to discourage you

ALSO BORN ON THIS DAY: Filmmaker Cameron Crowe; actor Harrison Ford; actor Patrick Stewart

The Crab

July 14 · **Cancer** · You are quick-witted, highly verbal, and prone to react in a haughty manner when crossed. You may seem very social and fun-loving, but you are considerably more serious than your personality makes you appear. You are dedicated to public expression of your opinions. Whether or not others believe in what you have to say is not really of any great concern to you. As long as you have a means of expressing yourself, you're content. If you do receive some measure of praise or acceptance for your beliefs, it's icing on the cake.

AVOID: Feelings of inferiority; inertia; doubts

ALSO BORN ON THIS DAY: Filmmaker Ingmar Bergman; actor Matthew Fox; musician Woody Guthrie

July 15 · **Cancer** · You often look to relationships to tell you who you are because you understand better than most people what the harmonics of day-to-day relationships signify. You are sensitive, yet strong. You have a powerful attraction to beauty in all its aspects and seek to replicate it in your own life. Despite your charming personality, you are extremely sensitive and easily hurt. You have a knack for attracting individuals who can teach you the lessons you really need to learn in life. Because you understand relationships, you are especially suited for the counseling and social work fields.

AVOID: Overwork; destructive behavior; grumpiness

ALSO BORN ON THIS DAY: Journalist Arianna Huffington; football star/actor Alex Karras; artist Rembrandt

The Crab

July 16 · **Cancer** · Although quiet, introspective, and seemingly shy, you have a strong will and an innate sense of self. You have a commonsense approach to life: You hope for good things to happen but are never surprised when the opposite occurs.

AVOID: Isolation; lack of commitment; feeling blue

ALSO BORN ON THIS DAY: Comedian Will Ferrell; baseball star "Shoeless" Joe Jackson; actor Barbara Stanwyck

July 17 · **Cancer** · You are committed to excellence and achievement. You possess a high sense of honor and are a stickler for truth. Although you may have a decided weakness for flattery, you lack self-assurance and often hide behind a facade of sophistication.

AVOID: Procrastination; judging others; self-righteousness

ALSO BORN ON THIS DAY: Comedian Phyllis Diller; U.S. naval hero John Paul Jones; actor Donald Sutherland

July 18 · **Cancer** · You are gifted and unusual, and your unofficial motto is "just go for it." You get as much fun from participation as you do from victory. You have a competitive streak, but it's competition itself—not the result—that turns you on.

AVOID: Abandonment fears; inaction due to bewilderment; self-blame

ALSO BORN ON THIS DAY: Astronaut/U.S. senator John Glenn; South African president Nelson Mandela; baseball executive Joe Torre

The Crab

July 19 · **Cancer** · People born on this date are quiet and inscrutable, with a deeply sensitive nature. You possess a generally sweet temperament and a true love of people; in return, you're easy to love. You don't try to grab the spotlight, though you may be thrust unwillingly into it because of a colorful accomplishment or dramatic heroism. You want to feel good about yourself, and you're usually able to achieve this by doing your best in everything you attempt and refusing to allow yourself to obsess over failure. You realize that everyone has challenges in life and that the difficult times lead to important learning opportunities.

AVOID: Belligerence; attitude problems; moodiness

ALSO BORN ON THIS DAY: Artist Edgar Degas; guitarist Brian May; politician George McGovern

July 20 · **Cancer** · You have an extremely strong sense of justice; integrity is everything to you. Although critical by nature, you never seem self-righteous. And although you love to get your own way, you understand the power and importance of compromise. You have a gentle yet determined nature. You possess a loving heart, and because of this you can see the positive side of any situation. You are an excellent friend with an extraordinary concern and sympathy for the people you love. You are extremely talented but are unlikely to realize your potential unless you have the approval and support of others.

AVOID: Wallowing in self-pity; negative thoughts; feeling shy

ALSO BORN ON THIS DAY: Model Gisele Bündchen; musician Carlos Santana; actor Natalie Wood

The Crab

July 21 · Cancer ·
You are torn between a need to be conventional and a desire to be original. You often use your larger-than-life personality to conceal your sense of insecurity. At the core of your being, you are extremely sensitive and may suffer much more than is apparent to others. Outwardly, you appear to believe in yourself and in your goals, yet a small core of doubt may reside deep in your heart. Although you may know intellectually that you have what it takes to succeed, emotionally you may be quite needy, requiring the validation of a friend or loved one.

AVOID: Destructive behavior; bad moods; fatalism

ALSO BORN ON THIS DAY: Novelist Ernest Hemingway; actor Don Knotts; baseball star C. C. Sabathia

July 22 · Cancer ·
You are intellectually brilliant but overly emotional at times. Your sharp wit and sharper tongue get you into more than your share of verbal scrapes with loved ones. You are a bold individual who goes to great lengths to prove your abilities. Your edgy charm makes you appealing, yet your personality can be an acquired taste. You know how to impress others with very little effort. Your dreams are limitless. When you see the vast potentials and opportunities open to you, you're challenged to go as far as your abilities will take you. You have old-fashioned values and believe that anything worth having is worth working hard to obtain.

AVOID: Bias; gossip; being too critical of others

ALSO BORN ON THIS DAY: Actor Willem Dafoe; fashion designer Oscar de la Renta; game show host Alex Trebek

The Lion

July 23 · Leo · Like most Leos, you love being the center of attention. You love to tell jokes and use words in an unusual and memorable way. You do your homework: Whether working on a personal or a job-related project, you are always prepared. You're friendly and sociable, and you have the heart to transform a frivolous relationship into one that is deep and satisfying. You never stop working toward your goals. Although you may change direction, you start out waiting for that brass ring to come around, and when it does, you grab for it with enthusiasm.

AVOID: Being too analytical; mental exhaustion; looking back

ALSO BORN ON THIS DAY: Novelist Raymond Chandler; actor Philip Seymour Hoffman; U.S. Supreme Court Justice Anthony Kennedy

♌

July 24 · Leo · Optimism, unerring and eternal, is the keynote to your personality from childhood to old age. You're unwilling to acknowledge the possibility of failure, which is appropriate because you nearly always succeed. You have personality to spare and are often the center of attention among your friends. You like to surround yourself with plenty of happy people who know how to have a good time. You live in a benign universe where all the pieces of the cosmic puzzle eventually fall into place. Because of this, you're unlikely to approach your goals in a linear, organized fashion.

AVOID: Instability; disrespect for authority and order; escapism

ALSO BORN ON THIS DAY: Aviator Amelia Earhart; musician/actor Jennifer Lopez; pianist Peter Serkin

♌

The Lion

July 25 · Leo ·

You are one of a kind—a true trailblazer. You have a bold attitude toward life, and you may seem overly ambitious to people who do not understand you. You have a fascinating brand of intelligence that is rooted in the subconscious and allows you to deal with people on many levels. You are a leader, and for this reason the friends you choose are often awestruck followers. Although you have the ability to reach the top with little effort, you can also be your own worst enemy; an inability to follow through on your aims can spell failure. With proper motivation, you can achieve anything.

AVOID: Attitude problems; dishonesty; fear of failure

ALSO BORN ON THIS DAY: Actor Barbara Harris; model Iman; football star Walter Payton

July 26 · Leo ·

You have the genius to become an archetype in your field. It's not only that you possess amazing star quality and an intriguing personality, but you also have the ability to draw attention to yourself without making an effort to do so. You often find yourself at the center of controversy. You identify strongly with the downtrodden and choose as friends people who do not possess your advantages. You want very much to make a place for yourself in the world. You desire the material benefits that come with success, but more than that you want to enjoy the respect of your peers and colleagues. You will work tirelessly to achieve your goals.

AVOID: Boasting; manipulation of others; bad temper

ALSO BORN ON THIS DAY: Filmmaker Stanley Kubrick; actor Helen Mirren; playwright George Bernard Shaw

The Lion

July 27 · Leo · You embody a duality that is evident only to those who know you well. You appear to be entirely at peace with your emotional landscape, yet you possess a spiritual core of steel that allows you to "soldier on" no matter what is arrayed against you.

AVOID: Excessive impulsiveness; bad habits; isolation

ALSO BORN ON THIS DAY: Baseball star/manager Leo Durocher; Olympian Peggy Fleming; baseball star Alex Rodriguez

July 28 · Leo · You understand the value of your own singularity. Haughty yet lovable, you possess a personal code of ethics and a strong belief system. You have a great need to win, and you often hide your emotional vulnerability behind this showy aspect of your personality.

AVOID: Selfishness; greed; arrogance

ALSO BORN ON THIS DAY: Cartoonist Jim Davis; poet Gerard Manley Hopkins; First Lady Jacqueline Kennedy Onassis

July 29 · Leo · People born on this day are intensely focused. You like to be involved in all levels of every endeavor, and you are always willing to learn a little more about your world and the people in it. You are quite set in your ways and aren't likely to be swayed except by someone with exceptional skills of persuasion.

AVOID: Intolerant people; shyness; inattentiveness

ALSO BORN ON THIS DAY: Filmmaker Ken Burns; TV journalist Peter Jennings; musician Martina McBride

The Lion

July 30 · Leo · You are creative in a spiritual as well as a tangible sense. Your almost otherworldly nature is fortified by a pleasant personality and a strong sense of self. Although you occasionally seem aloof, you have a great love for humanity and a genuine charisma that draws others to you. You possess a singular charm that sets you apart. Although you are a loner by preference and temperament, you are intensely devoted to your friends. Your circle of pals is made up of people you love deeply. One of your major goals is to gather as much knowledge as you can. You have a great need to work with creative, exciting concepts.

AVOID: Fatalism; manipulation of others; intimidation

ALSO BORN ON THIS DAY: Novelist Emily Brontë; guitarist Buddy Guy; baseball legend Casey Stengel

♌

July 31 · Leo · You are a natural trendsetter who has the ability to sway others to your way of thinking. You are creative, friendly, and full of great ideas. You never play it safe; you put yourself out on a limb at every occasion to prove the worthiness of your positions. In more cases than not, your self-confidence and risk-taking are validated. You like diversity because it gives you the chance to discover fresh points of view. You have great enthusiasm for life. You're as excited about meeting personal goals later in life as you were when you were very young.

AVOID: Willfulness; instability; foolish choices

ALSO BORN ON THIS DAY: Business tycoon Mark Cuban; economist Milton Friedman; novelist J. K. Rowling

♌

The Lion

August 1 · Leo · People born on August 1 have heightened
sensibilities, with a style that reflects their inner and outer natures.
You have a lovable character and great potential. Your well-
developed ego tells you just how special you are; you tend to set
your sights very high, and you occasionally come across as haughty.
You want the validation of others, but you are not likely to sacrifice
your true self to that aim. Once you set yourself a goal, you doggedly
pursue it. You have a real genius for creating interesting and
fulfilling relationships that have positive effects on your life and the
lives of the people closest to you.

AVOID: Crass behavior; intolerance; poor personal choices

ALSO BORN ON THIS DAY: Musician Jerry Garcia; novelist
Herman Melville; designer Yves Saint Laurent

August 2 · Leo · You have an edgy, unique personality that
makes you interesting to others. Like many Leos, you believe there is
no such thing as having too many friends. Naturally, you enjoy being
the center of attention, but because you dominate the spotlight in
such a genteel and good-natured way, no one seems to mind. You see
no barriers to making your goals come true. Your outgoing, joyous
personality lends itself to success as a model, performer, or attorney.
You want it all, and you have the chance to achieve your dreams if
you keep your enthusiasm at a high pitch.

AVOID: Antagonism; bad money habits; regrets

ALSO BORN ON THIS DAY: Novelist James Baldwin; actor Myrna
Loy; actor Peter O'Toole

The Lion

August 3 · Leo · You have star quality and are extremely
ambitious. You work tirelessly toward your goals and do whatever
you can to better yourself educationally and professionally. You
possess great personal charm. Despite an appearance of self-
absorption, you are deeply committed to causes that benefit others.

AVOID: Family discord; jealous friends; overindulgence

ALSO BORN ON THIS DAY: Football star Tom Brady; actor Martin
Sheen; domestic diva Martha Stewart

August 4 · Leo · You have considerable personal magnetism
and an engaging personality. However, you are highly rebellious and
may have a hard time fitting into a conventional mold. You prefer to
do things your own way.

AVOID: Rash decisions; empty promises; arrogance

ALSO BORN ON THIS DAY: Musician Louis Armstrong; U.S.
President Barack Obama; author Helen Thomas

August 5 · Leo · You are intelligent and witty, with a flair
for good conversation and a fine sense of humor. You are generally
good-natured and love to be around other people. You have a
tendency to be obsessively dogmatic about your ideas.

AVOID: Egotism; forcing ideas on others; misjudging people

ALSO BORN ON THIS DAY: Astronaut Neil Armstrong; basketball
star Patrick Ewing; filmmaker John Huston

The Lion

August 6 · Leo · You are even-tempered and pleasant. You
have a talent for making friends, and you enjoy the social aspects
of friendship but are more concerned with putting down emotional
roots that will last a lifetime. You are exceptionally ambitious, and
from an early age you feel the need to live up to your own potential.
Although it may be hard for you to get your act together, once you
set yourself a path you follow it. You are constantly looking for a way
to train your talents and bend yourself toward something important
and interesting. Happiness and personal security are your major
goals.

AVOID: Willfulness; putting demands on others; self-pity

ALSO BORN ON THIS DAY: Comedian Lucille Ball; actor Robert
Mitchum; basketball star David Robinson

August 7 · Leo · You are mysterious and somewhat
enigmatic. You like to make great mysteries of even the smallest
things and refuse to live your life according to convention. You have
a magnetic personality and an unabashed need to play mind games.
Friendships can be rewarding for you as long as you feel comfortable
enough with your pals to express your deepest feelings. Your dreams
and goals can be as hard to define as you are. You are not usually
materialistic, and therefore you tend to be most interested in goals
that are spiritually oriented.

AVOID: Dark thoughts; revenge; selfish motives

ALSO BORN ON THIS DAY: Spy Mata Hari; radio personality
Garrison Keillor; actor Charlize Theron

The Lion

August 8 · Leo ·
You are a graduate of the proverbial school of hard knocks. Although you may seem unemotional or even distant, you are simply self-disciplined and in control of yourself. You are often forced to climb the hard road to success, but you wouldn't have it any other way. You want to earn every opportunity you receive and achieve success one step at a time; you look for no shortcuts. You are a great role model for your friends—by representing the marriage of talent and discipline, you are the envy of all who know you.

AVOID: Saying "I told you so"; a superior attitude; bitterness

ALSO BORN ON THIS DAY: Tennis star Roger Federer; actor Dustin Hoffman; swimmer/actor Esther Williams

August 9 · Leo ·
You are strong-minded, possessing the grit and ability to come back from difficult circumstances. You have a basic need to be challenged because it helps you to prove yourself on all levels of existence. You have great personal dignity and carry yourself in a royal fashion. You are immaculate in your grooming habits and are always conscious of looking your best in any situation. You are extremely proud and may even seem vain, though your friends understand it's just a pose. You have boundless ambition and immeasurable integrity—two qualities that aren't often found in a single individual. You handle this dichotomy with amazing skill.

AVOID: Repetition; health risks; insecurity

ALSO BORN ON THIS DAY: Basketball star Bob Cousy; poet Philip Larkin; football/baseball star Deion Sanders

The Lion

August 10 · Leo · You are a study in contrasts. Although you
have talents and resources that mark you as different, even unique,
your greatest wish is to be a part of the crowd. You have leadership
skills, and yet you know you have the best chance to achieve
personal goals through group activities.

AVOID: Underachievement; laziness; undue pride

ALSO BORN ON THIS DAY: Actor Antonio Banderas; U.S.
President Herbert Hoover; actor Norma Shearer

August 11 · Leo · You have an analytical intelligence that
prompts you to wonder how things work. Often quiet and reserved,
you may seem distant and aloof, yet you are actually sensitive and
caring. You have amazing patience.

AVOID: Emotional walls; delays; being too practical

ALSO BORN ON THIS DAY: Actor Viola Davis; writer Alex Haley;
Apple computer cofounder Steve Wozniak

August 12 · Leo · You require a great deal of personal
freedom. You generally know exactly what you want out of life and
don't know the meaning of the word quit. You go after your personal
and professional aspirations with everything you've got. You also
know how to bring out the best in others.

AVOID: Stubbornness; self-importance; being defensive

ALSO BORN ON THIS DAY: Filmmaker Cecil B. DeMille; musician
Mark Knopfler; tennis star Pete Sampras

The Lion

August 13 · Leo ·
Eccentric and philosophical, you possess a kinetic energy that is the envy of all who know you. You have the ability to make a name for yourself in anything you attempt. Challenges seem to awaken your fighting spirit and give you the inspiration you need. Despite your loner mentality, you have a wide variety of friends. You seek friendship more for the satisfaction it gives you to observe human nature than for its emotional rewards. You want to live life on your own terms. You gravitate toward the unique, the strange, and the unusual.

AVOID: Holding grudges; a condescending attitude; immaturity

ALSO BORN ON THIS DAY: Filmmaker Alfred Hitchcock; golf star Ben Hogan; activist Lucy Stone

♌

August 14 · Leo ·
Part mystery, part open book, you are perplexing, infuriating, and different. You usually manage to keep your true self carefully hidden from even your closest friends. This is a subtle defense mechanism that allows you to retain your autonomy without sacrificing the illusions held by others. Your charm effortlessly attracts people to you. Everyone will feel as if they know the "real" person, yet almost no one actually does. You do not rely on a succession of moves or a planned strategy to achieve your goals. You believe that fate, rather than effort, determines your future.

AVOID: Attempting to rewrite the past; lack of confidence; vengeful thoughts

ALSO BORN ON THIS DAY: Actor Halle Berry; basketball star Magic Johnson; actor/comedian Steve Martin

♌

The Lion

August 15 · Leo ·
August 15 men and women have enormous leadership potential. Though they may seem egotistical, they are simply savvy about their own abilities. You feel you have many lessons to impart to others. You see the big picture better than almost anyone and yet can appreciate the value of details. Unafraid of failure, you never limit your goals. You don't allow yourself to see any impediment to your success. Although your level of ambition may seem awesome to some, those who know and understand you expect nothing less.

AVOID: Exhibiting a prickly personality; rudeness; dominating others

ALSO BORN ON THIS DAY: Actor/filmmaker Ben Affleck; French Emperor Napoleon Bonaparte; actor Jennifer Lawrence

♌

August 16 · Leo ·
You live your life with the volume turned up. You're dedicated and disciplined and have a strong sense of personal destiny. Although you absorb and listen to the criticism of others, it rarely causes you to change your game plan. You are quite concerned with your personal image and create a persona for yourself that is very much at odds with your true nature. It isn't characteristic for you to believe in luck—good, bad, or otherwise; you believe in making your own luck. You manage your goals on two separate levels: "dreaming" and "doing."

AVOID: Stifling your true self; rudeness; a domineering attitude

ALSO BORN ON THIS DAY: Filmmaker James Cameron; actor Steve Carell; musician/actor Madonna

♌

The Lion

August 17 · **Leo** · You are highly focused and always follow
your own path; you're seldom influenced by trends. Although
personable, you have an aloof quality. You appear steady and
unflappable to others, but there are, in fact, times when your
emotions get the better of you and your thinking is scattered.

AVOID: Brooding; anger; bad attitude

ALSO BORN ON THIS DAY: Actors Robert De Niro, Sean Penn,
and Mae West

♌

August 18 · **Leo** · You have a penchant for taking chances
and get a thrill out of living dangerously. You have no hidden
agenda—you know what you want and don't try to hide the fact.
Your boldness is part of your attractiveness, which is heightened by
your natural charm.

AVOID: Foolish risks; confrontation; irresponsibility

ALSO BORN ON THIS DAY: Actor Robert Redford; actor Shelley
Winters; journalist Bob Woodruff

♌

August 19 · **Leo** · You have big dreams and enjoy pushing
yourself to the limit, both physically and mentally. You may have
some awkward years before you decide how to focus your energies,
but once you put it all together there's no stopping you.

AVOID: Temper tantrums; mood swings; petulance

ALSO BORN ON THIS DAY: Fashion designer Coco Chanel;
U.S. President Bill Clinton; writer Ring Lardner Jr.

♌

The Lion

August 20 · **Leo** · Although you are outwardly affable and genuinely sweet, you also have a dark side. You like keeping secrets, even from those closest to you. You are extremely sensitive, and you inevitably feel the disappointments and sadness of those you love as keenly as you feel your own.

AVOID: Alienation; coldness; inability to compromise

ALSO BORN ON THIS DAY: Actor Joan Allen; musician Isaac Hayes; novelist Jacqueline Susann

♌

August 21 · **Leo** · You are a practitioner of conspicuous consumption, and you don't make any apologies about it. You are jovial and friendly, with a winning personality that endears you to others. You have a great love and respect for learning.

AVOID: Bragging; selfishness; heeding advice from others without really thinking it through

ALSO BORN ON THIS DAY: Bandleader Count Basie; basketball star Wilt Chamberlain; musician Kenny Rogers

♌

August 22 · **Leo** · You have personal charm and plenty of class. High-strung and somewhat nervous, you thrive on attention from others, but you need to learn to believe in yourself. You are intensely loyal to your friends.

AVOID: Heeding inner fears; pettiness; moodiness

ALSO BORN ON THIS DAY: Novelist Ray Bradbury; chef Giada De Laurentiis; musician John Lee Hooker

♌

The Virgin

August 23 · Virgo · You are a guileless, genuinely nice
person with a mercurial, kinetic charm that brings you great
affection from others—and it doesn't hurt that you're constantly
looking after other people's happiness and welfare. Your graceful
bearing combines with a light touch of sophistication. You achieve
your goals in an orderly, practical manner. You learn from every
experience and use those lessons to your own best advantage in
future situations. Because of your enthusiastic nature, you never lose
faith in your own ability to make things happen. If your goals are
sidetracked, you look at it as a chance to regroup rather than as a
misfortune.

AVOID: Stubbornness; stress; burning the candle at both ends

ALSO BORN ON THIS DAY: Basketball star Kobe Bryant; actor/
dancer Gene Kelly; actor Shelley Long

August 24 · Virgo · You are a real lady or gentleman.
You are known for your excellent manners, good disposition, and
the generosity you display to those closest to you. Your greatest
challenge is remembering to be yourself. Because you may not have
a lot of confidence in your abilities, you often look to colleagues or
friends for validation. Your innate shyness makes it hard for you to
put yourself "out there," but with the encouragement of good friends,
you're more likely to give it a try. You are a doer, and you will never
stop trying to achieve your dreams.

AVOID: Belligerence; selfish motives; pettiness

ALSO BORN ON THIS DAY: Comedian Dave Chappelle; actor
Marlee Matlin; baseball star Cal Ripken Jr.

The Virgin

August 25 · **Virgo** · You have a complicated nature. On one hand, you seem to derive a great deal of emotional sustenance from the approval of those close to you. Yet you also qualify as a true pioneer who is not afraid to accept the personal and professional challenges that come your way.

AVOID: Being weighed down by regret; finding fault; worrying

ALSO BORN ON THIS DAY: Actor Sean Connery; tennis star Althea Gibson; TV personality Regis Philbin

♍

August 26 · **Virgo** · Quiet and introspective, you possess a strong sense of purpose. You have a great devotion to fairness and a desire to apply your energies for the benefit of others. You don't make a show of yourself in any way, and you prefer that others not attempt to put you in the spotlight.

AVOID: Transitory relationships; worry; prejudice

ALSO BORN ON THIS DAY: Politician Geraldine Ferraro; musician Branford Marsalis; Mother Teresa

♍

August 27 · **Virgo** · You use your creative abilities to advertise a particular point of view. You are deeply concerned with all of your responsibilities. Bold and determined, you have a social conscience and often involve yourself in projects that help others.

AVOID: Grudges; a wounded heart; jealousy

ALSO BORN ON THIS DAY: U.S. President Lyndon Baines Johnson; comedian Paul Reubens; actor Chandra Wilson

♍

The Virgin

August 28 · Virgo ·

You have a strongly creative nature that needs to be addressed. You grasp the interdependence of nature and art—you have a sensitive side that's complemented by inner strength, which helps you deal with life's demanding challenges. You have a good self-image and plenty of self-confidence, but you can be deeply hurt by others' bad opinion of you. Your biggest strength is your ability to know what you really want out of life, and you are never satisfied with just "getting by." You want to improve your mind, body, and soul in every aspect.

AVOID: Pretentiousness; cynicism; indifference

ALSO BORN ON THIS DAY: Comedian/actor Jack Black; Olympian Scott Hamilton; musician Shania Twain

August 29 · Virgo ·

You have a strong life force that's keenly expressed through your emotions. You have the potential to lead an extraordinarily spiritual life, though you must come to grips with all aspects of your personal relationships before this can be accomplished. You need to follow your own path, and you will experience setbacks and disappointment if you allow yourself to be influenced against your better judgment. You are not very adventurous, and you are likely to befriend individuals who are much like you. Because you are so emotional, you experience profound joy and sadness.

AVOID: Insecurity; self-criticism; compliance

ALSO BORN ON THIS DAY: Actor Ingrid Bergman; musician Michael Jackson; actor Isabel Sanford

The Virgin

August 30 · Virgo ·

People born on August 30 tend to have such a positive attitude about life that setbacks and delays don't slow them down. You have a high level of self-confidence and can envision success even before it happens. You have an overwhelming urge to express your individual identity, and you are known for your discriminating good taste. You have a great love of learning, travel, and the written word. Although you seem calm on the surface, you're actually high-strung and excitable. You're extremely fun-loving and enjoy a vibrant social life. You are a sincere friend and like to spend time with good pals.

AVOID: Ego issues; self-criticism; compliance

ALSO BORN ON THIS DAY: Investor Warren Buffett; novelist Mary Shelley; baseball star Ted Williams

♍

August 31 · Virgo ·

You have a showy yet tasteful personality, and you bask in the approval of others. Although you are original and intelligent, you are often impractical. Your eclectic tastes display erudition and a great deal of originality. You often find yourself in unusual circumstances; this suits your love of adventure quite well. You show your unique nature through the friends you make. You may not think of yourself as being especially goal-oriented, but you go after things in a big way—but often without making the necessary plans or considering details. You are able to see things from a wide perspective and to appreciate eccentricity and inventiveness.

AVOID: Confusion; domestic upheavals; hasty actions

ALSO BORN ON THIS DAY: Educator Marva Collins; educator Maria Montessori; musician Van Morrison

♍

The Virgin

September 1 · Virgo · You have a practical approach to
life that enables you to get things done. You take great pride in your
ability to organize your activities, and although you keep up a steady
pace with every project, you never hurry. To you, honest effort
equals success.

AVOID: Overwork; being too serious; solitude

ALSO BORN ON THIS DAY: Novelist Edgar Rice Burroughs;
musician Gloria Estefan; actor/comedian Lily Tomlin

♍

September 2 · Virgo · You need to feel that you're in
control. You are practical, serene, organized, and have exceptionally
good leadership potential. You can always see the humor in things,
though you don't often show that side of yourself to the world.

AVOID: Bad habits; lack of focus; repeating mistakes in love

ALSO BORN ON THIS DAY: Football star/analyst Terry Bradshaw;
actor Mark Harmon; actor Salma Hayek

♍

September 3 · Virgo · Highly ambitious and incredibly
goal-oriented, you may be fortunate enough to achieve your ultimate
goals early in life. You don't believe in limitations and will pursue
your dreams with every bit of energy and vitality you possess.

AVOID: Loneliness; predictability; boredom

ALSO BORN ON THIS DAY: Musician Al Jardine; novelist Alison
Lurie; Olympian Shaun White

♍

The Virgin

September 4 · **Virgo** · You are unique and independent-minded and march to the beat of a different drummer, often displaying extraordinary bravery in the simple act of living your life. You want to know the truth about yourself, whether positive or negative. Even though you have a great deal of common sense, you are also a natural risk-taker. Every day seems to beckon to you with new dreams and new goals. You never stop being excited by life and all its myriad experiences. You have a strong curiosity about everything that surrounds you, and you will continue to look for answers as long as you live.

Avoid: Fixation; obsessive love; incompatibility

Also born on this day: Radio broadcaster Paul Harvey; musician Beyoncé; novelist Richard Wright

♍

September 5 · **Virgo** · You stand out in a crowd. Smart and composed, you are usually in control of your emotions, no matter how severe your circumstances may be. Relationships are the very essence of life for you, and you spend your entire life working to make them the best they can be. Friends have a way of becoming family, while family members become true friends. Although you may satisfy yourself after attaining modest goals, it's not because you can't appreciate the big picture. Rather, it defines your notion that everything you put your hand to must be treated with equal conscientiousness and respect.

Avoid: Dependence; irrationality; mood swings

Also born on this day: Outlaw Jesse James; actor/comedian Bob Newhart; actor Raquel Welch

♍

The Virgin

September 6 · Virgo ·

You live life on the edge. You are not concerned for your physical safety and don't hesitate to take chances, including—sometimes—foolish ones. You have a strong spirit and a gentle nature, along with a great love for beauty in all its forms. You incorporate that characteristic into your life, work, and relationships. You want to live the good life: Style, art, and all things beautiful speak to you in a language few people understand. Self-discipline is not your greatest strength, and some of your goals may have to wait until you can learn to become more organized and aggressive.

AVOID: Indecisiveness; impatience; emotional neediness

ALSO BORN ON THIS DAY: Activist Jane Addams; actor/comedian Jane Curtin; musician Roger Waters

September 7 · Virgo ·

Although you may seem docile on the surface, you have a volatile inner energy that you use in pursuit of achievement. You are extremely ambitious yet never ruthless. You believe in playing by the rules and will not change your attitude no matter how badly you want success. You may seem to clamor for your place in the spotlight, but you prefer security to unpredictable excitement. Because you are typically a loner, you don't make friends easily. Your shyness may make you seem snobbish or aloof, though you are actually in great need of finding people who understand you.

AVOID: Single-mindedness; self-praise; anger

ALSO BORN ON THIS DAY: Musician Buddy Holly; filmmaker Elia Kazan; artist Grandma Moses

The Virgin

September 8 · **Virgo** · You are an inveterate searcher of truth. You are determined to get to the heart of things. Your practical view of life allows you to withstand difficulties without losing faith in yourself or your objectives. You may have a hard time connecting with those who see life differently than you do.

Avoid: Feelings of betrayal; destructive thoughts; brooding

Also born on this day: Comedian Sid Caesar; musician Patsy Cline; actor Peter Sellers

♍

September 9 · **Virgo** · You are a perfectionist, which often makes your life difficult and infuriates everyone around you. You put pressure on yourself, not so much to succeed but rather to be the best in your own eyes. You don't wait for opportunity to knock on your proverbial door—you go out and seize it.

Avoid: Bickering; scheming; undeserved pride

Also born on this day: Musician Otis Redding; novelist Leo Tolstoy; actor Michelle Williams

♍

September 10 · **Virgo** · You have a winning personality that makes you incredibly appealing to others. You are able to project your inner self through your charisma. You prize the intangibles of life, such as relationships, integrity, and learning.

Avoid: Fear of change; making demands; irrational choices

Also born on this day: Actor Colin Firth; fashion designer Karl Lagerfeld; baseball star Roger Maris

♍

The Virgin

September 11 · Virgo ·

Although you may seem excessively emotional, you're actually very centered; you know exactly what you wish to accomplish in life. Because your belief in yourself is strong and unwavering, you are able to withstand criticism. You possess an extraordinary sense of loyalty toward your friends, and you will go to extremes in order to make your loved ones happy and secure. You know you must sacrifice to make certain dreams come true, yet you never put your goals ahead of the people who are important to you.

AVOID: Temptations; ambition; dependence

ALSO BORN ON THIS DAY: Filmmaker Brian De Palma; football coach Tom Landry; novelist D. H. Lawrence

♍

September 12 · Virgo ·

You are much more jovial and relaxed than the typical Virgo. You are naturally happy and habitually look on the bright side. Nothing gets you down for long. You seek to put your resources to work helping others. Whether you possess a great deal of material wealth or only a nominal amount, you always find a way to give something to an individual who has less. Friends are one of the most important factors in your life. You draw a great deal of inspiration from your pals and may serve as a counselor or confidante.

AVOID: Showing off; need for constant approval; personal fulfillment at the expense of others

ALSO BORN ON THIS DAY: Musician/actor Jennifer Hudson; musician George Jones; Olympian Jesse Owens

♍

The Virgin

September 13 · Virgo ·
You do not typify the usual Virgo traits of caution and conservatism; you're more likely to walk on the wild side. You are a style setter in your own way. You have a cool and collected attitude that marks you as a winner. Your ability to make others feel comfortable and confident in any social situation is indicative of your natural talent as a host or hostess. A loner by temperament, you try to surround yourself with quirky, interesting people. You prize independence, originality, and the ability to be yourself in any social or personal situation.

AVOID: Conceit; envy; being overly sensitive

ALSO BORN ON THIS DAY: Actor Claudette Colbert; author Roald Dahl; filmmaker Tyler Perry

♍

September 14 · Virgo ·
You embody the true spirit of Virgo perfectionism. You have extraordinarily high standards and refuse to settle for second-best. Complex and seemingly demanding, you can be difficult to live with, but no one can doubt your sincerity. Friendship is not just a simple exercise in social involvement to you. It is a real and serious commitment. You have a humanitarian streak and want to make an important contribution to society. You aspire to perfection and feel insecure about your efforts if you fall short of that mark. One of your goals is to harmoniously balance the professional and personal sides of your life.

AVOID: Stubbornness; fear of commitment; stress

ALSO BORN ON THIS DAY: Actor Clayton Moore; filmmaker Hal B. Wallis; musician Amy Winehouse

♍

The Virgin

September 15 · Virgo · You have a natural talent for
communicating with others. You are scrupulously truthful, yet you
need to find a personal dream world that allows you an escape from
the harshness of reality. You have a sensitive nature that may at times
be obscured by your sparkling personality.

AVOID: Inflexibility; being judgmental; pleasure-seeking

ALSO BORN ON THIS DAY: Novelist Agatha Christie; actor
Tommy Lee Jones; filmmaker Oliver Stone

♍

September 16 · Virgo · You have a deeply spiritual nature
that sustains you in times of trouble and confusion. Although you
tend to be very steady, others may view you as vulnerable and even
fragile. You are not generally competitive, preferring to score a
personal best rather than a victory over someone else.

AVOID: Instability; unrequited love; solitude

ALSO BORN ON THIS DAY: Actor Lauren Bacall; actor Peter Falk;
musician B. B. King

♍

September 17 · Virgo · You are a fighter who doesn't
understand the concept of giving up. You take life seriously,
approaching each obstacle as a challenge. You are loyal and steadfast,
with real grit, and you remain true to your ideals no matter what.

AVOID: Possessiveness; superficial relationships; fatalism

ALSO BORN ON THIS DAY: Actor Anne Bancroft; basketball star/
coach Phil Jackson; musician Hank Williams Sr.

♍

The Virgin

September 18 · Virgo · You have great self-control and
an ability to use your energies for valuable achievement. You are
dedicated to self-sufficiency and don't like to rely on others. You are
serious and mysterious, going about your life with quiet precision.
You have an inability to trust any but those closest to you and
may discreetly promote yourself as enigmatic, even eccentric. You
prefer to keep your own counsel, yet when you discover someone
you can trust, you're immensely grateful to have a confidante. You
understand how to put all of your resources into getting what you
want out of life.

Avoid: Passivity; deception; secrecy

Also born on this day: Physicist Jean Foucault; actor James
Gandolfini; actor Greta Garbo

September 19 · Virgo · Few people possess your
charming personality and physical elegance. You always take great
care in how you present yourself, both physically and in the general
tenor of your actions, so that what people see is a sleek and refined
package. Although you like being the center of attention, you can
never be called an egotist. You are a lifelong student who never loses
interest in the mystery and beauty of life. If you can overcome your
vulnerabilities, you can accomplish anything you wish. Your ability
to believe in yourself is the key factor.

Avoid: Aloofness; isolation; excessive practicality

Also born on this day: Novelist William Golding; actor
Jeremy Irons; actor Adam West

The Virgin

September 20 · **Virgo** · You are the ultimate professional
in all you do. Practical and organized, you participate actively in life.
You are a doer, not a watcher. You are so frank and earnest about
achieving your desires that you may appear to be opportunistic, but
you're just being honest about your feelings.

AVOID: Blunt speech; emotional bullying; disapproval

ALSO BORN ON THIS DAY: Basketball coach Red Auerbach;
hockey star Guy Lafleur; writer Upton Sinclair

♍

September 21 · **Virgo** · You are quiet and personable. You
have a tremendous fear of failure and may sometimes hold back.
The ability to cross that divide is a real stretch for you, but when you
make it, you empower yourself as never before.

AVOID: Procrastination; easy answers; self-indulgence

ALSO BORN ON THIS DAY: Musician Leonard Cohen; musician
Faith Hill; novelist H. G. Wells

♍

September 22 · **Virgo** · Your powerful personality exerts
considerable influence over others. Although you may be drawn to
scholarly pursuits, you almost always find yourself in demand to
fulfill more worldly aims. You like to be at the center of activity.

AVOID: Shiftlessness; abandonment issues; a need for validation

ALSO BORN ON THIS DAY: Actor Bonnie Hunt; baseball manager
Tommy Lasorda; novelist Fay Weldon

♍

The Scales

September 23 · Libra ·
Individuals born on this date combine a love of learning with good taste—the hallmark of the Libra sign. You are an energetic fact-finder who tirelessly seeks answers to life's difficult questions. You have a friendly, outgoing disposition that commands the love and respect of others, and you manage to project an image of seriousness while maintaining your personal charm. Although others may think you are indecisive, it is simply your nature to weigh all aspects of a question before making a decision. Not only do you possess a wonderful sense of social decorum, you also cultivate deeply satisfying friendships.

AVOID: Irresponsibility; arguments; mental exhaustion

ALSO BORN ON THIS DAY: Musician Ray Charles; sculptor Louise Nevelson; musician Bruce Springsteen

September 24 · Libra ·
People born on this day are dynamic, artistic, and luxury-loving. Possessed of a charming personality and a subtle intelligence, you are far more complicated than you seem to be. Although your professional achievements give you a great deal of emotional fulfillment, you experience most of your satisfaction—and a great deal of your pain—from your personal relationships. To achieve the goals you set for yourself, you must bring your common sense into line with your intelligence. You want the world to value your talents yet before this can happen, you must become accountable to yourself.

AVOID: Restlessness; appeasement; dissatisfaction

ALSO BORN ON THIS DAY: Novelist F. Scott Fitzgerald; football star "Mean Joe" Greene; puppeteer Jim Henson

The Scales

September 25 · Libra · You have a strong sense of
personal honor and integrity. You are sharply focused and expect
a great deal of yourself. Opinionated and ethical, you are highly
motivated to achieve success on both worldly and spiritual levels.
And then there's a dark side that few people glimpse—that is, your
tendency to brood. You favor a small but select circle of friends and
aren't given to confiding in others. Although you are interested in
exploring the full spectrum of your own nature, this can be difficult
for you because you are sometimes afraid of your own intensity.

AVOID: Limitations; complicated relationships; brooding

ALSO BORN ON THIS DAY: Novelist William Faulkner; poet
Shel Silverstein; actor Will Smith

September 26 · Libra · You are a study in contrasts and
contradictions. You possess a sympathetic nature yet have a strong
will. Self-disciplined and practical, you are also extremely romantic
and given to periodic flights of fancy. Romance is serious—not
superficial—to you. You value a strong partnership that has more
going for it than mere physical attraction. Although you appear
reserved, you have a wonderful sense of humor that can diffuse any
problem or touchy situation. You are a self-starter who can set a task
for yourself and rely on the results. Goal-oriented, you work hard to
make your dreams come true, taking pride in a job well done.

AVOID: Inhibitions; restrictive measures; false hopes

ALSO BORN ON THIS DAY: Poet T. S. Eliot; fitness guru Jack
LaLanne; tennis star Serena Williams

The Scales

September 27 • Libra • You see life as a battle to be won.
You are determined, scrappy, and much more physically energetic than the average Libra. You live very much on the surface of things, never afraid to show your emotions. While you can seem a bit pugnacious at times, you never lose your sense of fairness.

AVOID: Extreme frugality; dogmatism; mistrusting others

ALSO BORN ON THIS DAY: Actor Wilfred Brimley; actor Gwyneth Paltrow; baseball star Mike Schmidt

September 28 • Libra • You love being in the spotlight.
You have an effusive, natural charm that you often use to achieve your aims in life. When you maintain good work habits and patience, you have won half your battle toward any career goal.

AVOID: Narcissism; a fickle heart; superficial love affairs

ALSO BORN ON THIS DAY: Actor Brigitte Bardot; actor Marcello Mastroianni; TV host Ed Sullivan

September 29 • Libra • You are a deeply sensitive person
who enjoys keeping secrets. You relate very well to others on a one-on-one basis but may have trouble getting along with them in a larger forum. You have the typical Libra charm, although you don't always possess the confidence to exhibit it.

AVOID: Superstition; negativity; cynicism

ALSO BORN ON THIS DAY: "The Singing cowboy" Gene Autry; physicist Enrico Fermi; journalist Gwen Ifill

The Scales

September 30 · Libra · You appear to be emotionally detached and aloof, but your personality resembles a volcano under an iceberg. With all your good grooming and perfectionist tendencies, you seem to have it all together, but you are actually much more explosive than you appear. You are not as easy-going and accepting as most Libras—in fact, you can be headstrong. You have an incredible appetite for life. You work hard, play hard, and never stop striving. You are incredibly focused on achievement and are willing to put all else on hold while you are involved in a project that's important to you.

AVOID: Being overly critical; pretentiousness; rivalries

ALSO BORN ON THIS DAY: Novelist Truman Capote; actor Deborah Kerr; musician Johnny Mathis

October 1 · Libra · People born on October 1 have a bold and uncompromising spirit and an ability to come back from hard times. Drawing upon this strength gives you great satisfaction because it allows you to demonstrate your true mettle to others. You enjoy being in the spotlight yet have far too much grace to appear egotistical or vain. You understand the need to build your future on the successes of the past. You seek harmony in all aspects of life and have an instinct for making the right decisions in both personal and professional matters.

AVOID: A domineering temperament; disapproval; petty people

ALSO BORN ON THIS DAY: Musician/actor Julie Andrews; U.S. President Jimmy Carter; actor George Peppard

The Scales

October 2 · Libra · People born on October 2 have
personality plus. You are extremely charming and attractive to the
opposite sex, you take real pride in your appearance, and you have
a strong sense of style. You identify with the finer things in life and
have a great capacity for learning. Even though you may seem to be
concerned with the more superficial aspects of life, you are actually
devoted to friendship and other essentials. You are a sensitive type
who doesn't like to be in an environment that is noisy, ugly, or in any
way unpleasant.

AVOID: Destructive impulses; self-righteousness; rages

ALSO BORN ON THIS DAY: Indian leader/peace activist Mohandas
Gandhi; novelist Graham Greene; comedian Groucho Marx

October 3 · Libra · You have great poise and composure.
You are able to withstand difficult times without complaint and can
learn major life lessons without seeming to change in any noticeable
way. You are charming, and although you have a very healthy ego,
you're not vain. While you may show a hint of the typical Libra
frivolity, you possess great self-sufficiency and are incredibly
logical. Although you want to live the good life, you may not be
willing to bend all your efforts to this aim because you understand
that to be completely happy, you must give at least equal time to
your personal life.

AVOID: Worry; predictability; empty praise

ALSO BORN ON THIS DAY: Musician Chubby Checker; novelist
Gore Vidal; baseball star Dave Winfield

October 4 · Libra · Although Libra rebels are rare, you fall into this category. Of course—in the tradition of your sign—you are well-bred and polite, yet you're a rebel all the same. You have respect for tradition, but you make it a point to question social mores.

AVOID: Trends; lack of focus; gossip

ALSO BORN ON THIS DAY: Actor Charlton Heston; silent film actor Buster Keaton; actor Susan Sarandon

October 5 · Libra · You experience considerable conflict between your intellectual and spiritual goals. You value learning, yet you understand that it is experience that brings true wisdom. You pride yourself on your sense of social responsibility, yet you never allow your political ideology to get in the way of having a good time.

AVOID: Fear of change; an argumentative attitude; disinterest

ALSO BORN ON THIS DAY: Hockey star Mario Lemieux; actor/comedian Bernie Mac; actor Kate Winslet

October 6 · Libra · You are a dreamer with a great need to express your inner drive through imagination and creativity. You love fantasy and illusion and are less concerned with the reality of existence than with the essence of it. What appears to be true is much more interesting to you than what may actually be true.

AVOID: Frittering away time; escapism; unwise love

ALSO BORN ON THIS DAY: Anthropologist Thor Heyerdahl; actor Carole Lombard; inventor George Westinghouse

The Scales

October 7 · Libra ·
You need to come out of your emotionally protective shell in order to meet your real destiny. You have a strong philosophical bent, which you often express through humanitarian activities. You try to use whatever influence you possess to help others. Although your opinions are often extreme, you have the dedication and commitment necessary to make a difference. There is a dark side to you that may not be apparent to any but those closest to you. Because of your tendency to be moody on occasion, it's important for you to be involved in lighthearted, life-affirming activities.

AVOID: External pressures; nervous tension; sexual excesses

ALSO BORN ON THIS DAY: Comedian/talk show host Joy Behar; cellist Yo-Yo Ma; Archbishop Desmond Tutu

October 8 · Libra ·
You are a level-headed type who cannot be swayed by personal flattery. You possess the usual Libra charm, and the power of your personality is felt by all who know you. Still, you don't trade on this talent. You believe in paying attention to detail. You are personally ambitious yet care more for relationships than any professional enterprise; an ability to balance both is one of your trademarks. You have the ability to achieve your goals without any showiness or ego; you have the patience to take each day as it comes.

AVOID: Greediness; restriction; love of power

ALSO BORN ON THIS DAY: Actor/comedian Chevy Chase; actor Matt Damon; political leader Jesse Jackson

The Scales

October 9 · Libra ·
You have the natural gift of making peace. You possess a strong love of beauty and truth. Your unique and singular life is spent in the search for truth and in understanding both the material and spiritual aspects of your world. You are controversial yet good-natured. You may display a sharp wit in your debates with others, but you are more ironic than sarcastic. Whether or not you want to hear the truth, you will always ask for it. You need to feel you are living life on your own terms. You will gladly throw off all the trappings of status to get to a point where nothing matters except your personal autonomy.

AVOID: Impossible odds; making enemies; a foolish heart

ALSO BORN ON THIS DAY: Musician PJ Harvey; musician John Lennon; golf star Annika Sörenstam

October 10 · Libra ·
You play by the rules. You have a good sense of self and care a great deal about your personal reputation. Although you possess a pleasant temperament and a charming disposition, you lack a certain level of humility. Yet true to your Libran nature, you are never gauche enough to show it. You have the ability to command respect from others. You do this by exerting your own brand of subtle charm in ways that are completely irresistible. Because you need to feel as if you are constantly moving forward in life, you embrace change.

AVOID: Hesitation; dishonesty; hopelessness

ALSO BORN ON THIS DAY: Football star Brett Favre; actor Helen Hayes; pianist Thelonious Monk

The Scales

October 11 · Libra · You have the ability to put other people at ease. You have a sweet and sensitive nature, which in no way implies a lack of strength. In truth, you possess considerable grit and determination and are often drawn toward adventure despite being somewhat afraid of what it will bring.

AVOID: Emotionalism; inner fears; living in the past

ALSO BORN ON THIS DAY: Novelist Elmore Leonard; First Lady Eleanor Roosevelt; football star Steve Young

October 12 · Libra · There are few individuals who possess the sort of generous spirit that you display. You like living large, and you enjoy the respect of others. You are fun-loving, always looking for ways to have a good time with your many friends.

AVOID: Conflict; struggle; intemperance

ALSO BORN ON THIS DAY: Actor Hugh Jackman; musician Sam Moore; opera tenor Luciano Pavarotti

October 13 · Libra · You have enormous inner strength. You may have a fragile or quiet exterior, yet underneath that reserve you are pragmatic and loaded with common sense. You have the potential to be idealistic, yet you do not want to be caught off-guard. You are a true romantic at heart.

AVOID: Guile; inability to forgive; need to dominate others

ALSO BORN ON THIS DAY: Comedian Lenny Bruce; musician Paul Simon; British Prime Minister Margaret Thatcher

The Scales

October 14 · Libra · You incorporate the very best traits

of Libra. You are intelligent, diplomatic, and concerned with the sort of image you project to others. You have a flair for expressing yourself, and you are a master of communication. Although you may appear lighthearted on the surface, you are extremely serious at your core. You are introspective but still manage to display a warm personality. You are a good friend who believes in sharing all the joys and problems of life with the people you love. Because you have natural leadership abilities, you are often in the position of giving advice to pals.

AVOID: Mistrust; depression; unhappy love matches

ALSO BORN ON THIS DAY: U.S. President Dwight D. Eisenhower; actor Lillian Gish; basketball legend John Wooden

October 15 · Libra · You are a pleasure-seeking, luxury-

loving individual. These traits are generally assets, but there are times when they cause you to become your own worst enemy. You are always quick to apologize for your real or imagined misdeeds but, unfortunately, you go on living your life in a way that makes the recurrence of such actions not just possible but probable. Good-hearted but often misguided, you can get yourself in a real bind simply trying to be honest, only to discover that everybody else is playing by different rules.

AVOID: Pretense; social climbing; superficiality

ALSO BORN ON THIS DAY: Celebrity chef Emeril Lagasse; filmmaker/actor Penny Marshall; philosopher Friedrich Nietzsche

The Scales

October 16 · **Libra** ·
You are a peace-loving individual who nevertheless can meet tough challenges. You have an engaging, almost childlike, love of making spontaneous gestures. Further, you have the ability to judge others in a wise yet kindly way. You have a strong humanitarian streak and display a great deal of concern for the welfare of other people. Your sincerity and lack of pretense draw others to you easily. You have the ability to set specific goals for yourself without becoming obsessive. You have great organizational ability and know how to take a project one step at a time.

AVOID: Shyness; unrealized dreams; lack of fulfillment

ALSO BORN ON THIS DAY: Actor Angela Lansbury; musician John Mayer; writer Oscar Wilde

October 17 · **Libra** ·
Tortured and complicated, you understand the need to suffer to obtain wisdom. You must follow a circuitous route to your destiny, forced to learn important life lessons along the way. These are generally related to your relationships with others but include a great deal of personal soul-searching as well. You are savvy enough to realize that no matter how hard you work, you may not receive the acclaim or status you want. That rarely deters you because you are more concerned with your own efforts than the results. You realize that success is an arbitrary term.

AVOID: Scandal; impulsive actions; carelessness

ALSO BORN ON THIS DAY: Astronaut/doctor Mae Jemison; daredevil Evel Knievel; playwright Arthur Miller

The Scales

October 18 · Libra · You are dynamic, spirited, and energetic. Not as diplomatic as the average Libra, you refuse to sugarcoat your opinions. You are ambitious, even a little aggressive, but you wear it well. You are not afraid to display your confidence. You are a real self-starter who believes in taking control of your life.

AVOID: Recklessness; self-admiration; a quarrelsome nature

ALSO BORN ON THIS DAY: Musician Chuck Berry; football legend Mike Ditka; tennis star Martina Navratilova

October 19 · Libra · You find fulfillment through bringing together the worldly and the spiritual sides of your nature. You have strong yet flexible opinions on many subjects. You are curious about life and have a fierce love for learning.

AVOID: Preoccupation; dishonor; fickleness

ALSO BORN ON THIS DAY: Novelist John le Carré; actor John Lithgow; musician Peter Tosh

October 20 · Libra · You embody the yin-yang principle: Duality is your defining characteristic. Your attitudes, even your personality, may seem changeable, yet you are merely displaying both sides of your nature. In order to understand yourself, you must be willing to accept your dark side as well as your positive side.

AVOID: Illusion; arrogance; flamboyance

ALSO BORN ON THIS DAY: Composer Charles Ives; actor Béla Lugosi; baseball star Mickey Mantle

The Scales

October 21 · Libra · Smart, sassy, even a little sarcastic,
you know how to put your personality on display. You are bold and
creative, and you need your own space and aren't afraid to claim it.
You're fun-loving, a bit mischievous, and you don't mind breaking a
few rules now and then, stirring things up so that others take notice.
You demonstrate the antic demeanor of a typical Libra, but your
sense of emotional loyalty is very real. You like to do things your
own way and would rather fail at something than give up control of
your destiny.

AVOID: Empty praise; superficiality; frivolous ambition

ALSO BORN ON THIS DAY: Poet Samuel Taylor Coleridge;
musician Dizzy Gillespie; writer Ursula K. Le Guin

October 22 · Libra · You are definitely something special.
You combine personal charm with intelligence and talent. Although
you shine effortlessly in the spotlight, you are a natural loner who
draws strength from privacy. You want to make your mark on the
world and may even feel that you are destined to do so. Although
your expectations may strike others as being naive, you take in
all the possibilities available to you and ask "why not?" With your
optimism and enthusiasm, you don't put up any barriers to what you
can accomplish in life. If you want something, you go after it with
surprising tenacity.

AVOID: Loss of inspiration; looking back; dependency on mate

ALSO BORN ON THIS DAY: Physician Deepak Chopra; novelist
Doris Lessing; composer Franz Liszt

The Scorpion

October 23 · Scorpio ·

Individuals born on October 23 have the charismatic personality so often found in those whose birthday falls on the cusp between signs. You have a definite flair for putting yourself into situations where you will be noticed, but then you are just as likely to pull back, vexed, when too much attention is accorded to you. You think big. You are not interested in listening to the reasons why something cannot be done, only in how you can turn that negative into a positive. You enjoy living at a high pitch and would rather be in chaos than boredom.

AVOID: Being overly secretive; going to extremes; self-fulfilling prophecies

ALSO BORN ON THIS DAY: Talk show host Johnny Carson; TV host Nancy Grace; actor Ryan Reynolds

♏

October 24 · Scorpio ·

You have great personal magnetism. In love with life, you possess a highly romantic and sensual nature that defines your personality. You are extremely talented as well as fiercely competitive. You have a haughty disposition but are actually much nicer than you appear. You may have difficulty deciding just what you want out of life. Your talents often make things easy for you. Still, you want to strive, fail, then begin again: Only through this complicated scenario do you feel as if you've earned your place in the sun.

AVOID: Carnality; extravagant behavior; hidden agendas

ALSO BORN ON THIS DAY: Actor F. Murray Abraham; actor Kevin Kline; musician Bill Wyman

♏

The Scorpion

October 25 · **Scorpio** ·

For you, the past is never very far away. You compare each new experience to what you have known. In this way, you learn from your mistakes and are able to turn adversity into success. You don't believe in doing anything the easy way. With your extremely sensitive and highly imaginative nature, dreams and illusions are as concrete to you as reality. You expect your friends to be unflinchingly loyal and singularly devoted. There is a certain ageless quality about you. In youth you may seem far older than your years, while old age only seems to refine your unique qualities.

Avoid: Possessiveness; regret; addiction

Also born on this day: Musician Katy Perry; artist Pablo Picasso; actor Marion Ross

♏

October 26 · **Scorpio** ·

You are easy to love, yet hard to know. You value power and know how to use it, but you are more concerned with using it to help others rather than to glorify yourself. You are extremely self-disciplined. Personal honor means a great deal to you, and you are a fanatic about keeping your word. No one else in the world is more likely to keep a promise than you are. You are interested in wielding power, though usually from behind the scenes. You will go to great lengths to put your ideas out there for others to see.

Avoid: Wallowing in grief; being stymied by regret; obsessiveness

Also born on this day: First Lady/U.S. Secretary of State Hillary Rodham Clinton; game show host Pat Sajak; musician Keith Urban

♏

The Scorpion

October 27 · Scorpio · You are a complicated person
who likes to walk the tightrope between excitement and extreme risk. You can be sensible; you can be a daredevil. There's so much contradiction in your behavior that it's difficult to know how you'll react from one moment to the next—and that's the way you like it.

AVOID: Negativity; insecurity; being too demanding

ALSO BORN ON THIS DAY: Comedian/actor John Cleese; TV personality Kelly Osbourne; U.S. President Theodore Roosevelt

♏

October 28 · Scorpio · You are precise and dedicated to
doing a good job. You can become very disgruntled with yourself if you can't live up to your own expectations—which are occasionally too ambitious. You are tough on others and tougher on yourself.

AVOID: Dictatorial attitudes; perfectionism; willfulness

ALSO BORN ON THIS DAY: Software developer Bill Gates; Olympian Bruce Jenner; actor Julia Roberts

♏

October 29 · Scorpio · You are quixotic and spritelike, with
a changeable nature and an exciting personality. You always seem to be observing, rather than taking part. You dislike being the center of attention, even though you have the ability to draw the spotlight to yourself. You are the ultimate secret-keeper.

AVOID: Envy; blaming others; troublesome love affairs

ALSO BORN ON THIS DAY: Comedian Fanny Brice; actor Richard Dreyfuss; actor Winona Ryder

♏

The Scorpion

October 30 · Scorpio · You seek knowledge in order to
gain wisdom, and you have an adventuresome spirit that manifests
itself in a great love of travel and distant cultures. Although not
academically inclined, you think of yourself as a lifelong student.
You are an innovator in the way you live life, understanding that
in order to progress you must partake in new experiences. To
trust instinct over intelligence can be a challenge for you, but it is
generally a sound goal. Not only can you make friends with virtually
anyone, you are able to build up the self-esteem of others.

AVOID: Pretense; ambivalence; insensitivity to others

ALSO BORN ON THIS DAY: U.S. President John Adams; musician
Grace Slick; actor Henry Winkler

♏

October 31 · Scorpio · You are in search of truth and
spiritual oneness. You are not a rebel, but a loner, and you have
no need of validation from others. Although your personal life
may be characterized by highs and lows, you have tremendous
endurance and can always get past a disappointment or a setback.
Your forthright attitude allows you to display your honesty without
seeming brusque or harsh. You get along well with others but are
careful about enforcing emotional boundaries. You have great
spiritual potential and are continually striving to learn more about
yourself.

AVOID: Questioning existence; disorganization; promiscuity

ALSO BORN ON THIS DAY: Actor/musician Dale Evans; actor
Michael Landon; TV journalist Dan Rather

♏

The Scorpion

November 1 · Scorpio · November Scorpios are far

more intense than their late-October cousins, but those born on November 1 are somewhere in between. You have a restless, energetic spirit, yet you are far more people-oriented than many natives of your sign. You want your place in the sun and are constantly striving for success. Even when you meet with serious obstacles, you remain a survivor with big plans about how to turn things around. You look to your friends for inspiration and experience, and you never take friendship lightly.

AVOID: Negativity; apprehension; disenchantment

ALSO BORN ON THIS DAY: Music producer/composer David Foster; musician Lyle Lovett; model/actor Jenny McCarthy

♏

November 2 · Scorpio · You are a stubborn individual

with an incredible amount of emotional and spiritual stamina. Although you often seem quiet and somewhat introspective, you are a fighter who supports the status quo and expects it to support you. You are the king (or queen) of high drama. Every emotional scene in your life is like something out of an opera. You are not someone who enjoys being disagreed with; because of that, you often get your own way. You are intensely loyal to your friends and expect similar loyalty in return. You have high standards and want to do everything on your own.

AVOID: Dogmatic attitudes; hypocrisy; possessiveness

ALSO BORN ON THIS DAY: Actor Burt Lancaster; musician k. d. lang; U.S. President James K. Polk

♏

The Scorpion

November 3 · Scorpio · You are sarcastic, inventive, and extremely precocious. Your attitude of wry amusement seems to say that you know a few secrets about life that other people can't guess. Although you enjoy the good things that come your way, you never quite believe that your good luck will hold.

AVOID: Rivalries; a desire to rewrite the past; cynicism

ALSO BORN ON THIS DAY: Comedian/actor Roseanne Barr; actor Charles Bronson; baseball star Bob Feller

♏

November 4 · Scorpio · Your need to create controversy exerts its will in every aspect of your life. Quick-witted and talkative, you tell the truth without fearing its consequences. Eccentric behavior is the norm for people born on this date. You are the real article and will not deviate from your own standards for any reason.

AVOID: Tedium; feeling blue; looking back

ALSO BORN ON THIS DAY: TV journalist Walter Cronkite; actor Matthew McConaughey; actor Doris Roberts

♏

November 5 · Scorpio · You love things that can be proven by science. You are a natural student. You are constantly looking for answers, cultivating knowledge to better understand yourself. More than anything, you believe in being happy.

AVOID: Questioning authority; materialism; sarcasm

ALSO BORN ON THIS DAY: Musician Art Garfunkel; actor Vivien Leigh; actor/musician Roy Rogers

♏

The Scorpion

November 6 · **Scorpio** · You are a passionate, romantic

individual with the ability to communicate on many levels. Although relationships are the centerpiece of your life, you are nevertheless extremely self-sufficient. You may seem serious on the outside, but you know how to have a good time. You are a lover of luxury and enjoy having all the familiar creature comforts. When you feel blue, you have a tendency to pamper yourself. Honesty is the key to your relationships—you work very hard to make all of your personal relationships happy and honest.

AVOID: Secretive behavior; overwork; worry

ALSO BORN ON THIS DAY: Actor Sally Field; filmmaker Mike Nichols; TV journalist Maria Shriver

♏

November 7 · **Scorpio** · Very few people have the

potential you possess. You have intelligence and spirituality in equal measure—a marvelous combination. Although you possess a strong sense of mission in life, you are also profoundly inner-directed, needing a lot of time to concentrate on your personal sense of fulfillment. You take your friendships seriously and will keep your word to a friend without fail. Being a mentor as well as a pal is second nature to you. Because you are dedicated to spreading good in the world, you do your best work in jobs that give you the opportunity to help others.

AVOID: Absolutism; conflict; misunderstandings

ALSO BORN ON THIS DAY: Evangelist Billy Graham; musician Joni Mitchell; documentarian Morgan Spurlock

♏

The Scorpion

November 8 · Scorpio · You must walk your own path
in life, even if it is a difficult one, and you will usually resist help
at every turn. You prefer to give advice rather than take it. You
have a quirky vision that—though it may not align strictly with
reality—is definitely your own. If you are bold enough to divulge
that vision to others, you can be handsomely rewarded. You are
extremely secretive and have a hard time allowing other people to
be an intimate part of your life. You have amazing patience and can
withstand delays and disappointments like few other people.

AVOID: Compulsive behavior; spitefulness; disrespect

ALSO BORN ON THIS DAY: Novelist Margaret Mitchell; musician
Bonnie Raitt; chef/TV personality Gordon Ramsay

♏

November 9 · Scorpio · You are extremely adventurous,
energetic, and always on the lookout for new and interesting
experiences. You seem to be constantly in motion, continually
involved in new tasks and challenges. You have a definite need to
live life on your own terms. You never stop investigating the world
around you, and you don't mind making mistakes as long as you
learn from them. Because you understand that you cannot have the
sort of life you want without taking a few chances, you're more than
willing to work without the proverbial net.

AVOID: Risks; a defensive attitude; pipe dreams

ALSO BORN ON THIS DAY: Actor Lou Ferrigno; actor/inventor
Hedy Lamarr; astronomer Carl Sagan

♏

November 10 · Scorpio · You have so much strength of will that when you put your mind to it, there is nothing you cannot accomplish. You possess keen intelligence. You have a hard time deciding whether to pursue spiritual or material goals.

AVOID: Frivolity; weakness; squandering talents

ALSO BORN ON THIS DAY: Actor Richard Burton; writer Neil Gaiman; actor Ellen Pompeo

♏

November 11 · Scorpio · Unable to live life on a strictly material level, you depend upon knowledge and experience to take you where you wish to go. You have marvelous creative powers, which you put to use in even the most ordinary circumstances.

AVOID: Indulging inner fears; spending too much time on petty details; power trips

ALSO BORN ON THIS DAY: Actor Leonardo DiCaprio; actor Demi Moore; novelist Kurt Vonnegut

♏

November 12 · Scorpio · You possess a dual nature and may be perceived as either a saint or a sinner. You are essentially a loner, yet you have a magnetic personality that forces others to take notice of you. You can use your appeal in a manipulative fashion, though if you do, you run the risk of alienating others.

AVOID: Unkindness; selfish motives; vindictiveness

ALSO BORN ON THIS DAY: Actors Ryan Gosling, Anne Hathaway, and Grace Kelly, princess of Monaco

♏

The Scorpion

November 13 · Scorpio · Thanks to your powerful
conscience and strong desire for personal autonomy, you have the
ability to go against the "crowd." Uniqueness is so important to
you that you have been known to actually adjust your opinions to
deliberately conflict with those of others! You have a natural dignity
in the way you carry yourself. You are humorous, spontaneous, and
often lucky. You see things from a quirky perspective. You know the
level of your own talents, but no matter what you have to offer, you
will resist if you cannot do things your way.

AVOID: Irreverence; ill will; stress

ALSO BORN ON THIS DAY: Actor Whoopi Goldberg; filmmaker
Garry Marshall; author Robert Louis Stevenson

♏

November 14 · Scorpio · You are deeply introspective and
refuse to conform to the worldly standards of success. You have a
deep affinity for nature, and you are at your most spiritually fulfilled
when communing with it. You regard yourself in an abstract,
analytical way and often make objective judgments regarding your
motives and inner drives. Because you are extremely sensitive, you
may appear aloof, even snobbish. Your friends, however, know how
kind and considerate you truly are. You strive to achieve a spiritual
oneness with nature. This gives you the solace you need.

AVOID: Craftiness; immorality; unhappy heart

ALSO BORN ON THIS DAY: England's Prince Charles; artist Claude
Monet; U.S. Secretary of State Condoleezza Rice

♏

The Scorpion

November 15 · Scorpio ·

You are a fun-loving individual who enjoys being the center of attention. Your outward high spirits are something of a departure from the usual brooding Scorpio demeanor. You have the same level of intensity, but with a lighter touch. You like to feel that you are free to do anything you want in life. If you feel tied down or restricted in any way, you simply cannot be happy. You always look to get the most out of your personal relationships, but even if these turn unsatisfactory, you are unlikely to give up on happiness.

AVOID: Hysteria; gossip; perfectionism

ALSO BORN ON THIS DAY: Actor Ed Asner; musician Petula Clark; judge Joseph Wapner

November 16 · Scorpio ·

You have the ability to transcend your everyday experiences, gaining wisdom through encounters with others. You may seem wise beyond your years, even as a child. You have a solemn, almost stern attitude that makes you appear humorless, yet you actually have a wonderful personality. You are incredibly passionate and romantic. Your love bridges a void between the complex and the simple. You understand the spiritual aspects of love, and you judge with your heart more than your mind. You are always on a quest to get to the bottom of things. You want answers to everything.

AVOID: Frustration; notoriety; revenge

ALSO BORN ON THIS DAY: Actor Maggie Gyllenhaal; musician Diana Krall; actor Burgess Meredith

The Scorpion

November 17 · **Scorpio** · You carry yourself with great dignity. You have the rare ability to read the hearts and intentions of others. Your wisdom gives you a spiritual view of life; because of this you refuse to get caught up in anything superficial.

AVOID: Subjectivity; resentments; false friends

ALSO BORN ON THIS DAY: Actor/filmmaker Danny DeVito; actor Rachel McAdams; TV producer Lorne Michaels

♏

November 18 · **Scorpio** · You are vibrant and energetic, and you possess amazing determination and an unbeatable will. You have a need to put your personal stamp upon existence. Never satisfied with "the way things are," you seek to improve and even perfect yourself. You tend to try to control everything around you.

AVOID: Loss of faith; preoccupation with minor details; delays

ALSO BORN ON THIS DAY: Novelist Margaret Atwood; astronaut Alan Shepard; actor Owen Wilson

♏

November 19 · **Scorpio** · You are taciturn and likely to keep your own counsel. You have a powerful, almost magnetic presence that makes you a good leader, yet you do not mix well with others. One of your greatest talents is the ability to make other people feel good about themselves.

AVOID: Scarcity mentality; blunt remarks; injustice

ALSO BORN ON THIS DAY: Talk show host Dick Cavett; actor/filmmaker Jodie Foster; fashion designer Calvin Klein

♏

The Scorpion

November 20 · **Scorpio** · You are a complex and
complicated person who can be truthful to the point of recklessness.
You strive constantly for achievement, eager to prove that "good
guys" finish first. You are driven and gravitate toward high-powered
careers where you can make a difference in the world. Loyalty is
practically a religion to you—you make the best friend and the worst
enemy. You have great protective loyalty to those you love, but you
are quick to turn against those who hurt you or those close to you.
Although you dislike change, you are often instrumental in bringing
it about in the lives of others.

Avoid: Showmanship; bragging; harsh judgments

Also born on this day: U.S. Attorney General Robert F.
Kennedy; comedian/actor Joel McHale; actor Estelle Parsons

♏

November 21 · **Scorpio** · You are humorous and infinitely
practical. Quite simply, you're interested in getting the job done
and having a good time while doing it. You see yourself as a mover
and a shaker. A strong belief in your own skills and the ability
to see the big picture keep you actively involved in projects that
would intimidate other, less confident people. You are loving and
thoughtful and have a great desire to bring joy into the lives of
others. You are a hard worker with the common sense to know what
must be sacrificed for success.

Avoid: Hasty decisions; instability; pride

Also born on this day: Magazine editor Tina Brown; actor
Goldie Hawn; baseball star Stan Musial

♏

The Archer

November 22 · **Sagittarius** · You are fun-loving, yet you
have a serious side. You often put yourself on the line for the people
you love and the causes you value. You have so much class that it's
impossible for anyone to dislike you. November 22 people love to
travel and often find their truest friendships with people from other
cultures. You are a big dreamer, and you aren't likely to map out your
goals. You like to go where the wind takes you. You know how to
maximize your level of enjoyment in life, but you are wise enough to
know that material achievements don't always equal success.

AVOID: Procrastination; nihilism; divisiveness

ALSO BORN ON THIS DAY: Tennis star Boris Becker; novelist
George Eliot; actor Scarlett Johansson

November 23 · **Sagittarius** · You have a strong
conscience, though you enjoy flouting convention. You are able to
size up people and situations with ease. You are an idealist about
romantic love but can bounce back from heartbreak. You have
enormous leadership potential. November 23 individuals are often
excellent teachers, sports coaches, and motivational speakers.
Because you posses an entrepreneurial spirit, you often profit from
your own ideas. Accumulation of fortune is seldom your aim, but
you often accomplish it when you simply follow your best instincts.
You live in the moment and prefer not to pursue scenarios that
promise complications with minimal enjoyment.

AVOID: Ridicule of others; sarcasm; scattering energies

ALSO BORN ON THIS DAY: Chef Rick Bayless; actor Boris Karloff;
politician Chuck Schumer

The Archer

November 24 · **Sagittarius** · You have an exceptional
level of intelligence, yet you don't need to be identified with it for
purposes of ego. You have a need for many friends. You especially
enjoy people who have your gift for conversation and ideas. Love is
a romantic idyll for November 24 people. You often fall for someone
who is your opposite, and thus force yourself to deal with thorny
philosophical issues. Since you are often academically inclined, you
may overlook natural artistic abilities that may be relegated to the
role of hobbies. November 24 people make excellent chefs, writers,
and comedians.

AVOID: Escapism; impulsive behavior; self-doubt

ALSO BORN ON THIS DAY: Actor Katherine Heigl; basketball star
Oscar Robertson; artist Henri Toulouse-Lautrec

November 25 · **Sagittarius** · Individuals born on this
date are in a constant search to connect with others. Your spirituality
affects all your major decisions. It's virtually impossible for you to
look at things from an opportunistic point of view. Far from losing
out on success by this method, you manage to attract good things
into your life because of it. You have more followers than friends
because even though you are quiet, your spiritual aura is very
strong and leads others to depend upon you. Despite your spiritual
leanings, you have a rare gift for making and handling money. You
are incredibly generous.

AVOID: Resting on laurels; egotism; shallowness

ALSO BORN ON THIS DAY: Baseball star Joe DiMaggio; musician
Amy Grant; actor Ricardo Montalban

The Archer

November 26 · Sagittarius · You like to do things your own way. You are self-disciplined and centered. Your goal is ultimate wisdom. You have a great deal of emotional toughness and feel that only through hard work and difficulty can you truly regard yourself as being successful.

AVOID: Intolerance; pessimism; regrets

ALSO BORN ON THIS DAY: Musician Robert Goulet; cartoonist Charles Schultz; musician Tina Turner

November 27 · Sagittarius · There are few more independent thinkers than the people born on November 27. You inspire others with your explosive personal style. You are notorious for playing practical jokes. You are known to labor for long periods without allowing outside distractions to take away your focus.

AVOID: Superficial friendships; conceit; overspending

ALSO BORN ON THIS DAY: Author James Agee; musician Jimi Hendrix; martial artist Bruce Lee

November 28 · Sagittarius · You are an inspiration to others. You have a large circle of friends who are relatively unknown to each other. You make unusual career choices and change careers quite often because you have many and varied interests.

AVOID: Lack of commitment; banality; mistrust

ALSO BORN ON THIS DAY: Poet William Blake; actor Ed Harris; political satirist Jon Stewart

The Archer

November 29 · Sagittarius · You must learn to tell

yourself the truth in all things. Friends provide a mirror by which
you can decipher your own image. You are often unwilling to set
firm goals for fear you'll be unable to achieve them. This attitude
needs to be dispelled before any progress can be made. To boost
confidence, it is good for November 29 men and women to seek
out careers that give them opportunities to project their personality
through the work they do. Although you may be reticent to enter a
career in retail sales, real estate, or teaching, November 29 people
score high in all these pursuits after their first taste of success.

AVOID: Chaos; discord; impossible goals

ALSO BORN ON THIS DAY: Novelist Louisa May Alcott; actor Don
Cheadle; baseball star Mariano Rivera

November 30 · Sagittarius · You have a razor-sharp wit

and the personality of a stage star. Forging friendships is not easy
because you are extremely competitive. People born on this day have
unequaled sales skills, though they often favor another line of work.
Smart alternatives include comedy, education, law, advertising, or
writing. You have incredible luck with money, but gambling can be
a problem if you don't learn to resist the urge. November 30 natives
have so much talent and personal appeal that they may find their
goals come a little too easily. Many people born on this date are
underachievers for this very reason.

AVOID: Trendiness; conflict with authority; meddling

ALSO BORN ON THIS DAY: Politician Shirley Chisholm; actor/
comedian Ben Stiller; author Mark Twain

The Archer

December 1 · Sagittarius · You live life on your own

terms, which generally means very few rules. You see yourself as a glamorous figure and may at times favor a somewhat superficial approach to love. It takes someone really special to get you to settle down. You enjoy being in the public eye. You are not the sort who can labor behind closed doors; instead, you enjoy professions that enable you to make use of your sparkling personality. You find interesting careers in sales, advertising, or show business. Although you prefer spontaneity to setting goals, you do have a strong will and can achieve amazing things when you put your mind to it.

AVOID: Self-promotion; the dark side; controlling others

ALSO BORN ON THIS DAY: Musician/actor Bette Midler; actor/comedian Richard Pryor; golf star Lee Trevino

December 2 · Sagittarius · You are highly romantic

and greatly talented. You love on an epic scale. Although you seem strong, you are quite vulnerable. December 2 people believe that, with a little luck, any dream can come true. Few people display the loyalty and affection to friends that you do. You are capable of great insight, and for this reason your friends often come to you with confessions or questions. There is never any doubt concerning your sincerity. You often place your career goals above everything else. This is sometimes your way of coping with disappointments in other areas of life.

AVOID: Rash choices; envy; a broken heart

ALSO BORN ON THIS DAY: Opera diva Maria Callas; musician Britney Spears; designer Gianni Versace

The Archer

December 3 · *Sagittarius* · You thrive on the challenge of
pursuing love but may quickly lose interest. You have a bit of trouble
making an emotional commitment because you are likely to equate
it with giving up personal freedom, your most prized possession.
You tend to see the big picture rather than the small details.

AVOID: Frivolous romances; moodiness; belligerence

ALSO BORN ON THIS DAY: Novelist Joseph Conrad; artist Gilbert
Stuart; Olympian Katarina Witt

December 4 · *Sagittarius* · You are intense about your
personal freedom. December 4 individuals have a love of electronic
gadgetry and often look for career options in communications,
mathematics, or various scientific disciplines.

AVOID: Bad choices; misrepresentation; becoming sidetracked

ALSO BORN ON THIS DAY: Actor Jeff Bridges; musician Jay-Z;
actor Marisa Tomei

December 5 · *Sagittarius* · You are a dreamer and a
doer. Your challenge is to stay true to your ideas without being
intimidated by any negative feedback. Because you have an
incredible ability to accurately judge the taste of others, you have
great potential to market your own product or idea.

AVOID: Confusion; fear; daydreaming

ALSO BORN ON THIS DAY: Entrepreneur Walt Disney; musician
Little Richard; filmmaker Otto Preminger

The Archer

December 6 · **Sagittarius** · You are a kind individual

with a genuine love of people. You are a natural mediator. Your positive attitude and exquisite good manners make you nice to be around. You raise sociability to an art form. You are an old-fashioned romantic. If you suffer a broken love relationship, you need a significant period of time for healing. December 6 individuals often carry their mediating ability into adulthood. This talent makes them excellent lawyers, judges, and corporate executives. If you go into the education field, you have a great impact on students who might otherwise have little interest in schooling.

AVOID: Predictability; manipulation; mistakes

ALSO BORN ON THIS DAY: Filmmaker Judd Apatow; lyricist Ira Gershwin; comedian Steven Wright

December 7 · **Sagittarius** · Your great wisdom allows

you to perceive life on many levels. December 7 natives don't so much choose friends as are chosen as a friend by others. You have a natural ability to act as a counselor, and you often dispense advice. Although you have many talents, you gravitate toward work in the arts. December 7 natives make talented musicians, photographers, painters, and dancers. Because people born on this day feel strongly that to do something strictly for money is unethical, finances are a tricky factor in your life. Your idealism is laudable, but it needs to be tempered with a more practical attitude.

AVOID: Artistic pretensions; self-glorification; denial

ALSO BORN ON THIS DAY: Baseball star Johnny Bench; actor Ellen Burstyn; author Willa Cather

The Archer

December 8 · Sagittarius · Though you are usually
headstrong, you also have a docile side. Because you possess a
fascinating personality, you have no lack of people wanting to get
close to you. You use the force of your personality to further your
aims at work. December 8 folks are big spenders who enjoy showing
their generosity to loved ones. You like to gamble, and should
take care to monitor your emotional attachment to this pastime.
People born on this date have considerable integrity and will not
compromise it for personal gain. To them, winning counts only
when it's achieved fairly.

AVOID: Destructive behavior; impatience; being flattered too easily

ALSO BORN ON THIS DAY: Musician Nicki Minaj; musician Jim
Morrison; author James Thurber

December 9 · Sagittarius · Although you have a jovial
temperament, you also possess an edgy attitude that often draws
you into controversy. You enjoy surrounding yourself with a group
of people that knows how to have a good time. You may remain
single, usually for fear that any relationship will dissolve in boredom.
December 9 natives enjoy careers that allow them to travel. They
thrive in the hospitality business and make good teachers, tour
guides, or language instructors. You can be irresponsible in the way
you handle monthly bills. Still, your forgetfulness is one of your
charms. You have the resilience to bounce back from failure.

AVOID: Safety risks; deceit; excessive sarcasm

ALSO BORN ON THIS DAY: Football star Dick Butkus; actor Dame
Judi Dench; actor John Malkovich

The Archer

December 10 · **Sagittarius** · You believe in getting things done. If a mate doesn't respect the boundaries you put up, you may lose interest. December 10 individuals handle stress well and excel as surgeons, first responders, and air traffic controllers.

AVOID: Detours; negative vibes; disillusionment

ALSO BORN ON THIS DAY: Actor/filmmaker Kenneth Branagh; poet Emily Dickinson; chef Bobby Flay

December 11 · **Sagittarius** · Intellectually gifted, you have the ability to transform your world into something quite amazing. You need to believe in your ability to make the world a better place. Personal goals often revolve around travel and learning.

AVOID: Fixating on the past; contradictions; intimidation

ALSO BORN ON THIS DAY: Actor Teri Garr; musician/actor Rita Moreno; writer Aleksandr Solzhenitsyn

December 12 · **Sagittarius** · In romantic matters, you show a great deal of sophistication. Since friends are sometimes lovers and lovers are always friends, you remain friends with all of your exes. You are articulate and witty, and often choose to make your living with words. You are well suited to work in journalism, comedy, advertising, academia, and law.

AVOID: Defensive behavior; danger; scarcity

ALSO BORN ON THIS DAY: Writer Gustave Flaubert; painter Edvard Munch; musician/actor Frank Sinatra

The Archer

December 13 · Sagittarius · Eccentricity marks the
personality of people born on this day. When it comes to leadership
ability, you are second to none, though that sort of role seldom
appeals to your antic sense of fun. Even though you love having
people around, you believe that familiarity often breeds contempt.
You are totally honest in all your relationships. If you are unhappy,
you simply say so and move on. You are the original entrepreneur,
whose ideas are so far ahead of your time you can't help but succeed
or fail in spectacular ways. Your mind is in a constant state of flux,
churning out amazing—and sometimes impossible—concepts.

AVOID: Sensationalism; imitation; superficiality

ALSO BORN ON THIS DAY: Actor Steve Buscemi; actor
Christopher Plummer; musician Taylor Swift

December 14 · Sagittarius · You have the ability to
juggle a variety of tasks and responsibilities. While others may be
bemoaning a potential problem, December 14 people have already
worked it out and moved on. Men and women born on this date
never differentiate among a good friend, an old friend, or a best
friend. Friends simply are, and friends are what life is all about. To
be, to think, to do, to express—these are the goals of December
14 natives. You have little interest in putting together a linear plan of
life and achievement. If it feels good, if it helps someone, if it creates
beauty for even an instant, you are all for it.

AVOID: Stubbornness; lack of control; resistance

ALSO BORN ON THIS DAY: Actor Patty Duke; novelist Shirley
Jackson; politician Margaret Chase Smith

The Archer

December 15 · Sagittarius · December 15 men and
women are success-oriented, but they have far too much integrity to
ever go against their principles to get what they want. You constantly
look to your pals for advice. Romance can be complicated for you,
and you may endure more than your share of unrequited love. You
never lose hope, though. You are often drawn to semipublic work.
Retail sales is a particularly rewarding field for you, since it allows
you to make use of your people-skills and charming personality. You
have a strong work ethic and are delighted when rewards flow from
your efforts. You seem destined to easily draw money into your life.

AVOID: Mood swings; bad temper; tardiness

ALSO BORN ON THIS DAY: Comedian Tim Conway; industrialist
J. Paul Getty; novelist Edna O'Brien

December 16 · Sagittarius · You have such a disciplined
nature that you can live on very little, as long as you have the
opportunity to express your inner fire. You believe that success
equals creative accomplishment, not money. You have so much
wisdom that you may seem to be plugged in to some cosmic energy
source that the rest of the world can't see. You have a habit of
pushing people away, especially when you most need help. You listen
to your intuition rather than to conventional wisdom. You have high
expectations for your talent, yet are willing to allow it to develop at
its own pace. You believe that true art cannot be forced.

AVOID: Reclusiveness; indulgence; feelings of superiority

ALSO BORN ON THIS DAY: Novelist Jane Austen; composer
Ludwig van Beethoven; cultural anthropologist Margaret Mead

The Archer

December 17 · **Sagittarius** · December 17 individuals
have the vision and practicality to succeed in business. Your ability is
predicated upon a keen understanding of what the public wants. You
are likely to do well in graphics, catering, or pet care.

Avoid: Destructive habits; poor judgment; ruthlessness

Also born on this day: Conductor Arthur Fiedler; novelist
Ford Madox Ford; model/actor/musician Milla Jovovich

December 18 · **Sagittarius** · You want to wake up every
day eager to go to work. If your career can't support that level of
enthusiasm, you'll look for something that does. You don't believe
in putting limits on what you can achieve, but you don't expect
anything to come to you without a lot of hard work.

Avoid: Lethargy; indecisiveness; lack of commitment

Also born on this day: Baseball star Ty Cobb; musician Keith
Richards; filmmaker Steven Spielberg

December 19 · **Sagittarius** · You make friends
effortlessly. If you succeed very early in your career, you may lose
your edge. The more difficult the odds against you, the more likely
it is that you will triumph. You are happiest when you can use your
professional status to effect positive change.

Avoid: Insincerity; bias; disbelief

Also born on this day: Musician Édith Piaf; actor Cicely
Tyson; football star Reggie White

The Archer

December 20 · Sagittarius · You may struggle to break
free of the image others have of you. Once you learn to see yourself
as independent of your current situation, your true self can emerge.
December 20 natives choose friends they would like to emulate. You
have an old-fashioned view of romance and may seek to connect
with individuals who favor your happily-ever-after mentality. You
have a way of drawing resources into your life without even trying.
December 20 natives often choose professions that pick up the tab
for travel expenses. You are fascinated with the world around you
and look for ways to bring new experiences into your life.

AVOID: Needy people; fear of change; stifling your true self

ALSO BORN ON THIS DAY: Musician Billy Bragg; writer Sandra
Cisneros; filmmaker George Roy Hill

December 21 · Sagittarius · December 21 people often
lack self-confidence and need others to help them feel good. You
bring a high level of enthusiasm to your work. You need to feel
personally involved and able to make a difference in your world.
You have a talent for making good investment choices and are well
equipped to handle your own financial affairs. You have the ability
to reach the very top of your field once you learn to have confidence
in your abilities. Enormously talented, you can nevertheless be
hamstrung unless you appreciate your gifts. When you learn how
not to be your own worst enemy, your goals are apt to materialize.

AVOID: Depression; sense of loss; low self-esteem

ALSO BORN ON THIS DAY: Tennis star Chris Evert; Olympian
Florence Griffith-Joyner; musician Frank Zappa

The Goat

December 22 · Capricorn ·

You hide great sensitivity under a shell of pretended indifference. Although your circle of friends is likely to be small, you derive a great deal of happiness from relationships. You desire to love deeply but are afraid of the pain a broken relationship can inflict. It's only when you learn to trust your instincts that you find the perfect mate. December 22 people are likely to have a reputation for being workaholics. This isn't negative unless you are working hard to avoid issues related to relationships. December 22 natives are often shy about revealing their goals to anyone, preferring to keep them secret in case of failure.

AVOID: Guilt; selfishness; low self-esteem

ALSO BORN ON THIS DAY: Actor Ralph Fiennes; composer Giacomo Puccini; TV journalist Diane Sawyer

December 23 · Capricorn ·

You never blame your setbacks on anyone but yourself. If a goal becomes impossible to fulfill, you simply replot your course. Because of your good attitude and innate ability to motivate others, you make an excellent mentor. You are exceptionally verbal and often tell enjoyable stories. You make friends effortlessly. You value stability in life. You are very serious about your career ambitions. You work hard, learn quickly, and obey the rules. You spend a great deal of money on home decorating, with an eye for pieces that will increase in value as the years go on.

AVOID: Stress; demoralization; indifference

ALSO BORN ON THIS DAY: Football coach Jim Harbaugh; actor Susan Lucci; musician Eddie Vedder

The Goat

December 24 · Capricorn · You are totally unafraid

of being yourself at all times. You are different—and proud of it. You often have a secret agenda that you are unwilling to divulge to anyone, even your closest friends. You are an interesting combination of free-wheeling and conservative. You know that by alternating your methods, you're most likely to meet with success—and success is the goal of every December 24 native. For most, this has to do with business or career, but for others it can mean family life, personal power, or even a sense of spiritual enrichment. One way or the other, you hitch your dreams to a star.

AVOID: Irrationality; instability; self-destructive habits

ALSO BORN ON THIS DAY: Actor Ava Gardner; business magnate Howard Hughes; musician Ricky Martin

December 25 · Capricorn · You are drawn to life's

mysteries. You have an ability to read other people and understand their inner motives in a deep way. In romantic relationships, there is always a sense of the transitory, as if you aren't quite sure if you want to make things permanent. You are drawn to professions that allow you to indulge your love of knowledge. December 25 individuals make excellent lawyers, academics, and medical researchers. You are most likely to reach your goals if you have an emotional as well as material reason to succeed. If you experience a setback regarding a cherished goal, you are likely to try again, even harder, to achieve it.

AVOID: Laziness; lack of preparation; impossible odds

ALSO BORN ON THIS DAY: Musician Dido; baseball star Rickey Henderson; writer Rod Serling

The Goat

December 26 · Capricorn · December 26 people possess
a determined, exceptionally serious nature. The close friendships
formed by December 26 people remain part of their lives for
years. Romantically, you usually have your heart set on a firm
commitment, though you may fall in love with people who do not.
You are a meticulous, intelligent individual. You may seek to work
in a creative field, but in the role of a business or corporate figure.
December 26 people make excellent agents, corporate lawyers, and
accountants. Money is the centerpiece in the lives of December
26 people. This does not imply greediness, but rather a desire to see
that all your family members and loved ones are secure.

AVOID: Overconfidence; repression; an authoritarian attitude

ALSO BORN ON THIS DAY: Writer/composer/TV personality Steve
Allen; actor Jared Leto; novelist Henry Miller

December 27 · Capricorn · You elevate style to an art, yet
you are remarkably practical and down to earth. You tend to choose
friends who share your views and values. You are excellent at getting
others to work at their highest potential. December 27 natives are
about as good as it gets when it comes to handling money. Getting
to the top of your profession is a natural goal for you. Yet even your
ambition has a practical side. You know better than to ignore all
other aspects of life. You feel strongly that your existence is fulfilled
only if you can experience the joys of family life.

AVOID: Foolishness; temptation; inattentiveness

ALSO BORN ON THIS DAY: Actor John Amos; actor Marlene
Dietrich; chemist Louis Pasteur

The Goat

December 28 · Capricorn · You have great social skills,
including the ability to make anyone feel at home in any situation.
You take pride and enjoyment in performing everyday tasks,
believing that it is through the minor, not major, events in life that
character is formed and tested. You have a generally happy outlook
on life. You have a great capacity for friendship. You often choose
a career that puts you in the spotlight. You are sociable and do well
in a position of power. Those born on this date have a modest yet
earnest desire to do the very best they can. Your goals tend to be
carefully mapped out and may involve many years of trial and error.

AVOID: Artificiality; people who are only looking for fun; betrayal

ALSO BORN ON THIS DAY: Actor Maggie Smith; actor Denzel
Washington; U.S. President Woodrow Wilson

December 29 · Capricorn · You tend to experience a
great deal of emotional flux in your relationships. You sometimes
"freeze out" even your closest friends at one time or another because
of differences of opinion. An ability to bear down and get past the
fear that every relationship will fail is vital to your emotional well-
being. You have great creative talent and likely opt for a career in the
arts. You may feel vulnerable about your financial situation, even if
you make a good salary. This "scarcity mentality" can cause you to
make a few foolish decisions about money until you learn to move
beyond your fear.

AVOID: Sacrificial love; addiction; envy

ALSO BORN ON THIS DAY: Actors Ted Danson, Mary Tyler
Moore, and John Voight

The Goat

December 30 · Capricorn · You like the good life and are

willing to work hard to achieve it. You believe that no one can have
too many friends, and you enjoy making the social rounds. You want
a romantic partner who shares your philosophical and religious
beliefs. You have great leadership ability. Because of this and your
love of people, you make a wonderful supervisor or boss. You aren't
known for taking risks, but you will walk on the wild side if it means
a chance to experience something marvelous that will bring you
knowledge or pleasure. You have a genius for devising a balance
between your personal and professional lives.

AVOID: Preoccupation; self-indulgence; greed

ALSO BORN ON THIS DAY: Basketball star LeBron James; writer
Rudyard Kipling; golf star Tiger Woods

December 31 · Capricorn · You respond to the demands

of your heart, not your head. Because of your emotional intensity,
you experience a great deal of instability in your personal life.
This can be a drawback to your maturation. Although you have
an instinct to lead a stable, productive life, your emotions tend to
keep you from making good progress. You put feeling loved and
valued ahead of professional success. If you are able to conquer your
personal insecurities, you can be very successful in your career. You
have enormous creative talent, and if you have the opportunity to
tap into it, you are able to express your true self.

AVOID: Willfulness; flattery; ego issues

ALSO BORN ON THIS DAY: Olympian Gabby Douglas; actor
Anthony Hopkins; artist Henri Matisse